THE GOOD SPORT

PRAISE FOR *The Good Sport*

"Listening to Kevin White talk about his career in athletics is like taking a masterclass in sports management, leadership, and life. With wit, wisdom, and charm Kevin describes the challenges college athletics has faced over the past 50 years and helps us better understand what lies ahead. At this moment in the evolution of what it means to be an amateur athlete, we should listen to this man of unshakable character who has always put the welfare of student-athletes first."
– GEN (R) Martin E. Dempsey, 18th Chairman of the Joint Chiefs of Staff

"As a former student athlete, I have a strong appreciation for Dr. White's leadership. His decision making process was inclusive, as he was always willing to hear the opinions of others before making decisions. Dr. White leads by example and with a positive attitude. His best skill is his ability to clearly articulate his vision and a plan to achieve success. Dr. White's tutelage has rubbed off on many athletic departments across the country in intercollegiate athletics. I'm thankful for my time with Dr. White and the impact he had on thousands of student athletes during his career."
– Brady Quinn, Former Notre Dame Quarterback, Former NFL Quarterback, Football Analyst Fox Sports

"'Be bold' is the most treasured advice I received from Kevin White while working together to bridge the collegiate and Olympic/Paralympic landscapes. Kevin is a curious and courageous trailblazer, but more important than all of his accomplishments, is his calling as an empathetic educator. He encourages dreamers to aim for the stars and then helps his students reach them. Kevin's clever quips, parables and hilarious true stories not only drawn an audience, but leave a lasting impression. His advice is priceless and captured in his page-turner of a book. Thank you for 'being bold' and for dedicating your life to helping those around you pursue the stars!"

– Sarah Wilhelmi, Former United States Olympic and Paralympic Committee Senior Director of Collegiate Partnerships, and Teaching Professor at the University of Colorado, Colorado Springs

"Having worked for and been mentored by Kevin White at Notre Dame and Duke, I was fortunate to learn from one of the best leaders in the collegiate athletics industry. Kevin's book is a reflection of how his early life lessons formed the basis of his management style and the strategies by which he navigated through the ever-changing collegiate environment and culture. The book exudes his brilliance in managing complex daily practical and political college sports challenges. I will forever be indebted to Kevin for his generosity and patience in allowing me to learn from his vast experiences, knowledge and wisdom as I forged my own path within collegiate athletics administration. This book will give its readers a looking glass through which one can understand how and why Kevin White is one of the titans within the industry."

– Stan Wilcox, JD., Executive Vice President Regulatory Affairs, NCAA, Former Vice President and Director of Athletics Florida State University

"Kevin White is legendary in every sense of the word. Legends like Dr. White have stories of their accomplishments shared and told by many, many people. During our time here at Duke, we would not have had any chance to move the needle with the football program without the talent, drive, and work ethic of Dr. White. He is, without doubt, the most talented individual I've encountered during my career in athletics."

– David Cutcliffe, Special Assistant to the SEC Commissioner, Former DI Head Football Coach, Multiple Coach of the Year Award winner

"Kevin White's distinguished administrative career is one to be admired. He has successfully navigated the world of college athletics over four decades with professionalism, class and humility. He will go down as one of the best to ever lead an athletic department. I'm grateful for his belief in me as a coach and his positivity in the direction of our program. He is directly responsible for the varied successes of the Duke Athletic Department."
– Kara Lawson, Head Women's Basketball Coach Duke University

"When watching other teams you place a keen eye not only on the team but also on their administration. Because greatness starts top down. Kevin has always provided a great example and model of how this should be done."
– Tyrone Willingham, Former DI Football Head Coach, Former College Football Playoff Committee member

"For more than a decade, I loved working with Kevin White. He made Duke Athletics and Duke University so much better. In fact, he made the entire college athletics industry better. Kevin leads with his heart and never wavers from the strong values that define him as a person of the highest character. My family and I are incredibly grateful for his friendship, guidance, and the partnership our two families created together."
– Mike Krzyzewski, Former Duke University and United States Senior National Team Head Coach

"Kevin White tells the story of his amazing life and career in an impressively candid, introspective, and inspiring manner in The Good Sport. And what a fun read from a true master of his trade, the 'Mr. Clean of college athletics'. Reading about Kevin's roots, the many interesting characters in his early life, his career steps, his learnings along the way, how he applied those learnings to do ever better and more…we all benefit from his willingness to share them with us. Among his many, many strengths, Kevin is a true servant leader, an amazing developer of talent, and a champion of his

'customers' (college athletes and athletics)…things that are highly relevant for leaders in any field."
– Rick Wagoner, Retired Chairman and CEO, General Motors, Former Chair of the Duke University Board of Trustees.

"In my near decade with Kevin White I was always struck by his humility and willingness to listen to all sides before making a decision. Make no mistake he was our leader, but he always wanted input to make the best decision. I consider myself, and our family, lucky and blessed to have been so close with Kevin and Jane."
– Boo Corrigan, Director of Athletics North Carolina State University

"Kevin has all the traits of a great leader. Empathy, humility and an unwavering belief in his coaches. He had a way of expecting the best from you while continually helping you achieve your potential. He had the rare ability to know what to say, when to say it and also when to step back and listen. If you want to become a great leader, read this book!"
– Muffet McGraw, ESPN analyst, Former Head Women's Basketball Coach Notre Dame

"Kevin is an amazing leader and his ability to positively impact people, and the organizations they serve, is second to none. To be certain, I've been incredibly blessed to know Kevin as a friend, colleague and mentor for more than three decades. His endless support and advice have been priceless. He remains the 'gold standard' of college sports."
– ACC Commissioner Jim Phillips, Ph.D.

"Kevin White has been a dear friend and a trusted colleague throughout our careers. Dr. White has always demonstrated impeccable integrity, innovative vision, incredibly hard work and an unwavering commitment to the student-athlete. Kevin has served admirably in every role he has assumed,

whether as a volunteer or as a representative of his employer. I have always trusted Kevin to carefully consider issues, to thoughtfully make decisions and to rely on well-tested values to arrive at winning and highly principled results. He's a winner in every way."
– Bob Bowlsby, Vice President Bowlsby Sports Advisors, Former Big-12 Commissioner

"Kevin White has been a true North Star for college athletics for decades. As a practitioner and teacher, he has provided value-driven leadership based on integrity, dignity, and humaneness, coupled with extraordinary effectiveness. He is a shining example of how it should be done."
– John Swofford, Former Atlantic Coast Conference Commissioner

"Kevin White is a brilliant, articulate, and visionary leader who would have thrived in any sector, yet he devoted his career to higher education and more specifically intercollegiate athletics. Kevin's leadership, mentorship and friendship have changed the trajectory of thousands of lives throughout the intercollegiate athletics enterprise for the better, including mine. His relational skills are unmatched and his heart to pour into the next generation of college athletics leaders will leave an immeasurable legacy. Every leader or aspiring leader will benefit from reading about his journey."
– Ian McCaw, Vice President and Director of Athletics, Liberty University

"Kevin White is an extraordinary leader and person. He is team-oriented, and blends team goals with the professional development of every person in his charge. Kevin does a magnificent job of navigating change, and perhaps his greatest strength is listening. Kevin seeks input and thoughts from others, then makes an informed, "we first" decision. In the college sports industry, Kevin White is on its Mount Rushmore."
– Jay Bilas, ESPN

"Kevin White was a joy to work with during his years as Athletic Director at Notre Dame. He is the preeminent mentor of future athletic leaders in the country. He is also a terrific person and a treasured friend."
– Rev. Edward A. "Monk" Malloy, c.s.c., President Emeritus University of Notre Dame

"Kevin's leadership may be best evidenced by the human legacy of those who have been nurtured and empowered by him to lead their own great sport programs. I am certainly a better leader for Kevin's mentorship."
– Sarah Hirshland, CEO United States Olympic and Paralympic Committee

"Throughout his distinguished career in college athletics, Kevin White led with a clear vision and built strong relationships with stakeholders at every level. His secrets on effective leadership will be helpful for any aspiring leader."
– Adam Silver, NBA Commissioner

"Although our fourth president, John Quincy Adams, couldn't, of course, know Kevin White, he nonetheless described him perfectly: 'If your actions inspire others to dream more, learn more, do more, and become more, you are a leader.'"
– Chris Kennedy, Senior Deputy Director of Athletics and Adjunct Assistant Professor of English

"As an athlete, I've had the privilege of working with some incredible people but few have had the profound impact on my life and career as Dr. White. His unwavering dedication, vision and leadership have not only elevated Olympic sports but has also helped generations of athletes grow on and off the field. Dr. White understands what it takes to build champions and has

been instrumental in my success. I am tremendously proud to know him and witness his remarkable achievements."
– Abby Johnston McGrath, MD Duke Swimming & Diving '13, Olympic Diver '12 & '16

"Dr. White is the best leader I have encountered in collegiate athletics. I have seen his highly effective style through two lenses. As a former student athlete while at Notre Dame, and as a national media member at ESPN covering his Duke programs. I always marveled at his commitment to the well being of his student athletes and coaches, He had a supreme class and civility in his approach. He was relentlessly dedicated to nurturing those relationships and making those around him feel comfortable and cared for. That sincerity allowed him to seamlessly garner an unwavering support for his vision from those whom he led."
– Jordan Cornette, NBC Sports TV Personality, Former Men's Basketball player Notre Dame, Monogram Club Director

"Having served as Athletic Director in six different institutions and had his advice sought in many more, Kevin White is simply unparalleled in his knowledge of intercollegiate athletics. I'll go further: there may never be anyone, EVER, who knows this field better than Kevin. Add that he's a modest, low-ego guy who shows equal respect for everyone, holds himself and others to the highest ethical standards, and fights valiantly for his department while fully supporting the larger, non-sports mission of universities, and you begin to grasp how rare he is. Now we learn that this Irish storyteller is a natural writer too! Congratulations, Kevin, on this amazing tale."
– Richard Brodhead, President Emeritus, Duke University

"I knew from the 1st time I met Kevin White years ago that he would be going uptown in the world of intercollegiate sports . Kevin had all the qualities that are needed to become a 'Big Star' as an Athletic Administrator .

Yes, he possessed great enthusiasm, energy, knowledge, plus the golden gift as a master communicator. Yes, to me for decades KEVIN WHITE has been AWESOME BABY with a CAPITAL A!"
– Dick Vitale, ESPN

"In *The Good Sport* Kevin White takes us on his journey as an Irish Catholic kid growing up in 'blue-collar' Amityville on Long Island while scrabbling to help his parents make ends meet, to the position of 'the best of the best' among intercollegiate athletic directors of his generation. Along the way we discover the love and support White received from his parents and extended family and that he has passed onto his own kids as well as the enormous pride he takes in his Irish heritage. We also discover some of the 'whys' that have made White so successful: his ability to develop relationships; to identify precise strategic objectives; to understand the unrelenting need for resources to build intercollegiate athletic programs and the importance of team building to make it all happen. This book is both an interesting and delightful read."
– Roy Bostock, American Investor and Businessman, Former Duke Football and Baseball T'62

"Kevin has an extraordinary ability to motivate diverse constituencies toward a common goal. He has an uncanny ability to honor the dignity of everyone he meets while inspiring each to aspire and work toward something greater. Perhaps most uniquely, he cares for those with whom he interacts more than the larger purpose which might better benefit himself. Kevin exemplifies the character, integrity, and values of a world we desperately seek."
– Jim Collins, President Loras College

"Kevin is passionate, supportive, empathetic, inspiring and motivating—as a colleague, a friend, and a leader. My two years working directly with him allowed me incredible opportunities to expand my knowledge and

skills, and to grow within our industry. His vision and ability to anticipate future change helped me develop my own leadership style and philosophy. I have experienced first-hand Kevin's strong commitment to mentoring, and I appreciate that he has been willing to provide advice and guidance throughout my career."
– Bubba Cunningham, Director of Athletics University of North Carolina

"Kevin was an exceptional leader and role model. He consistently created opportunities for young people and offered unwavering support in their pursuits. His remarkable interpersonal skills and inspirational leadership set a high standard for us all. To this day, I still go to work each day and take the field, wanting to make him proud!"
– Marissa Young, Head Softball Coach Duke University

"Kevin White is the true embodiment of the servant leader. Throughout his distinguished career he has consistently modeled a commitment to family, dedication to each of his institutions and their causes. His integrity, humility and authenticity are unchallenged. All along his journey he has been focused on taking others along with him. His determination to make higher education, and the world at large, a more humanistic, kind and welcoming place to all, make him one of my favorite and most admired human beings of all time! Tip of the cap to the very best to ever do it!"
– Sandy Barbour, Huron Consulting, Former Director of Athletics Penn State

"Kevin White is widely recognized as the unofficial dean of university athletic directors. Some refer to him as 'the godfather' of intercollegiate sports. At latest count, Kevin has mentored 31 current athletic directors or other senior officials in collegiate athletics. He has been a perennial force— whether negotiating television rights for the then-PAC-10 Conference when he was at Arizona State University, representing Notre Dame to NBC, win-

ning two national championships in men's basketball at Duke, or serving on the United States Olympic Committee."
– Nathan Hatch, President Emeritus Wake Forest University

"Kevin White's track record of championship-caliber leadership in college athletics is unrivaled. He made everyone around him better with his unique ability to relate to student-athletes, coaches, and staff at every level of the organization. Duke University is fortunate to have benefited from Kevin's guidance and I am so grateful to call him both a colleague and a friend."
– Jon Scheyer, Head Men's Basketball Coach, Duke University

"Kevin's visionary leadership has transformed intercollegiate athletics programs around the country for decades. At the same time, Kevin's loyalty and investment in the student-athletes, coaches and staff around him has had an even bigger impact. I am excited that this book will be an extension of that work and have an even broader reach of Kevin's investment, care and support of the people working in intercollegiate athletics."
– Jim Sterk, Director of Athletics, Western Washington University

"Kevin's unique perspective on Life, Leadership and Education portrayed in *The Good Sport* will become a must read from board rooms to locker rooms to classrooms for many years to come. That perspective has been nurtured for over five decades as a student athlete, coach, administrator, and professor, in addition to earning a Ph.D while he and Jane raised 5 children on various campus communities across the country. Intercollegiate athletics has been blessed with phenomenal leadership through the years, but it would be difficult to identify an individual who has had as much of a holistic impact across the board than Kevin. I have been blessed to not only have a seat at Kevins table but have benefitted immensely by his tutelage."
– Bob Vecchione, CEO Emeritus NACDA

"No one person has had a stronger impact on college athletes in the last 30 years than Kevin. He's a humble servant leader who also happens to be an industry visionary. Kevin's impact will be felt for the next 100 years."
– Charles N Besser, Founder, President, CEO of Intersport

"Simply put, Kevin White is an icon! His leadership shined not merely through directives and decisions but in the way he elevated those around him. The 'consummate giver' with unwavering integrity, political acumen and strategic maneuverability, served as a beacon of light, illuminating the path for so many. With these morsels of lessons and reflections, Kevin's wisdom will be accessible to the masses—inspiring transformation in a way only a legend can."
– Allen Greene, Director of Athletics at The University of Pittsburgh, former MLB and Notre Dame Baseball player

"Kevin is a truly authentic leader, mentor, and friend. Over the course of his career as an educator, he launched the careers of many leaders, but part of what makes him unique is that he continues to serve as a sounding board and advisor to those he has inspired, generously sharing the wisdom he has acquired. I consider myself quite fortunate to be a small branch on the Kevin White tree, and I'm thrilled he is sharing his story, as I know it will be an inspiration to many others."
– Bernard Muir, Jaquish & Kenninger Director of Athletics at Stanford University

"Kevin's unparalleled experience as a leader and his tireless advocacy for student-athletes make him an invaluable part of the college athletics ecosystem. They also make his memoirs a 'must read' for college sports fans as well as students of leadership. We at Huron could not be more excited

to serve our college and university clients with Kevin as a core member of our team."
– Jim Roth, Vice Chairman of the Board of Directors and former Chief Executive Officer, Huron Consulting Group LLC

"Kevin White was and is the ultimate confidence giver. He had the 'Midas touch' on how and when to approach coaches, and after eight years working with him I do my best to emulate his leadership style with my staff. It was the honor of a lifetime to be the coach at Notre Dame for 23 years and I was so lucky to have Kevin in my corner. *The Good Sport* is the perfect roadmap on how to be a leader that is both effective and respected in everything they do!"
– Mike Brey, Assistant Coach for the Atlanta Hawks, Former Head Coach for Notre Dame Men's Basketball

"It is a great benefit to have the opportunity to learn from the long arc of a successful career and remarkable life. By sharing his story and perspective in The Good Sport, Kevin White brings us with him on a journey by combining the many highs with the reality of lessons learned the low points. The result is the kind of book that shares important insight, encourages provocative thinking, and provides a great example of what is accomplished by doing what is important when it is important."
– Greg Sankey, Commissioner of the SEC

"What a remarkable book. Kevin White's ascent from high school track coach to the pinnacle of college sports is itself remarkable. That he used simple, common-sense skills picked up from his parents, Emerson and Rita, or gleaned from his connection to the Irish diaspora, is even more remarkable. That he shared those secrets and those he picked up on the way is truly remarkable. Kevin White is an educator and mentor at heart and wants the reader to learn from his successes and failures. In this candid,

well structured, and superbly written account of his 40-year journey to the top, he reveals all and provides a road map for your success."
– Frank O'Mara, 3x Irish Olympian, 2x World Champion, Author of *Bend, Don't Break*

"Kevin White's career as an athletic director is unique and provides a window into the modern world of college sports. Leadership experiences at Maine, Tulane, Arizona State, Notre Dame and Duke provide the backdrop for Kevin's insights, anecdotes and analysis of the joys and challenges associated with life as a leader at five DI important programs over four dynamic decades. This firsthand account of a kid's rise from the neighborhoods of Long Island to the top of the college sports industry is worth the read for anyone who wants to take a ride with Kevin during his brilliant career."
– Jim Delany, Former Commissioner of the Big Ten

"Kevin White's legendary life journey has been a master class of working together to create long-lasting relationships and successful cultures in the intense world of big-time college athletics. *The Good Sport* is both entertaining and inspiring, a true road map for success."
– George Bodenheimer, Former President and Executive Chairman, ESPN

"From the moment I first met Kevin at Tulane, his unassuming yet confident demeanor and ability to instantly create relationships made him an undeniable leader. His book, *The Good Sport*, takes you inside the mind of one of college athletics' greats and provides sound advice for any aspiring leader!"
– Archie Manning

THE GOOD SPORT

Reflections *on a* Full Life *in* College Sports

Kevin M. White, Ph.D.

SBJ National Director of Athletics of the Year
Irish America Hall of Fame
NACDA Hall of Fame
Suffolk County Hall of Fame
St. Joseph's College Hall of Fame
Tulane University Hall of Fame
Loras College Hall of Fame
Amityville High School Hall of Fame

Copyright © 2025 Huron Consulting Group Inc

Published by:

Huron Consulting Services, LLC
550 W. Van Buren Street
Chicago, IL 60607
Phone: 312-583-8700
www.huronconsultinggroup.com

ISBN: 978-1-62218-116-2

All rights reserved. No part of this book may be used or reproduced in any form or by any means or stored in a database or retrieval without the prior written permission of the publisher, except in the case of brief quotations embodied in critical articles or reviews. Making copies of any part of this book for any purpose other than your own personal use is a violation of United States copyright laws. Entering any of the contents into a computer for mailing lists or database purposes is strictly prohibited unless written authorization is obtained from Huron Consulting Services LLC.

Printed in the United States of America

To my life partner of over 52 years, Jane White. A part of the original coaching duet, and the esteemed head coach of our family, I remain eternally grateful.

Also, to my late parents and grandparents, for I have endeavored to not let them slip completely away. This book was partially a motivation to perpetuate their individual stories.

Finally, to all the amazing student-athletes we coached and/or administered, over almost half a century, notwithstanding, the deeply treasured cohort of coaches, administrators, senior university administrators, trustees, and terribly generous benefactors, all of whom graciously supported my best efforts (and vision), I will be forever beholden.

TABLE OF CONTENTS

FOREWORD   VII
By Nina King, VP, AD, and Adjunct Professor of Business Administration at Duke

INTRODUCTION   1
A preview of the current turbulence throughout college athletics in America. And a reflection on the ways in which my story of origin and subsequent life experiences gave me what I needed to navigate a career in college athletics; embracing one's own unique existence and envisioning a destination of choice.

CHAPTER 1   11
Irish Ancestry: Inspiration

CHAPTER 2   23
Learning How to Play the Game: The Wilds of Long Island

CHAPTER 3   43
Developing a Career: Coaching Lessons and Reflections

CHAPTER 4   63
Loras College: Becoming the Leader

CHAPTER 5   77
University of Maine: Articulating the Vision

CHAPTER 6   91
Tulane University: Political Culture

CHAPTER 7   109
Arizona State University: Welfare of the Student-Athlete

CHAPTER 8   119
Notre Dame: Pluralism and Political Challenges

CHAPTER 9   145
Duke University: Philanthropy, Relationship and Leadership Imperative

CHAPTER 10   169
A Radical Shift: Reimagining the Future of College Athletics

EPILOGUE   185
The most important things for any Higher Education Administrator to understand about the purpose and goal of college athletics and the student-athlete experience.

FOREWORD

When I first stepped into the world of college athletics, I knew little beyond the excitement of the games themselves. I didn't yet understand the depth of leadership, the nuances of building relationships with a wide range of constituents, or the challenges that come with shaping a program that prioritizes both excellence and integrity while staying true to the university mission. But I was fortunate—very fortunate—to have a mentor who embodied what it means to be "The Good Sport."

This book, is more than just a collection of stories. It is a testament to the life's work of someone who not only led by example but took the time to pass on hard-earned lessons to those of us lucky enough to follow in his footsteps. I'm proud to say that many of the reflections in these pages mirror the lessons I've learned directly from Dr. Kevin White.

The world of college athletics is a unique arena where the passions of student-athletes and countless constituents, the pursuit of excellence, and the complexities of leadership intersect. For those who have spent their lives dedicated to this dynamic field, the lessons learned extend far beyond the playing fields and locker rooms. In this captivating read, legendary athletic director Kevin White takes us on an amazing journey through personal experiences, challenges, and triumphs that shaped his career in education and sports. This is a playbook showcasing the enduring values that define success in athletics and, more importantly, in life.

Many people across the college athletics landscape either know Kevin White or know of Kevin White. His vast experience and leadership style left a deep and lasting legacy at all of the institutions that he served, and beyond. Keep reading and you will *truly* learn who Kevin White is—from humble beginnings to a storied career, and everything in between. You'll gain insight into the proud family man behind the professional legend and the personal values that shaped his leadership, along with the challenges he faced along the way. This book takes you on a journey through the pivotal moments in Kevin's life, illuminating the passion, dedication, and resilience that defined his path. Whether you're familiar with his accomplishments or are hearing his story for the first time, you'll discover what makes Kevin White a remarkable figure in college athletics and beyond.

Moreover, Kevin shares an incredible amount of wisdom gained from over four decades of navigating the world of college sports. From the importance of mentorship and leadership to the power of resilience and adaptability, the lessons in this book resonate with anyone who has faced the demands of leading and managing the complexities of a competitive and changing environment. I've witnessed firsthand the impact of this wisdom on student-athletes, staff, and coaches—insights that go far beyond game strategy or winning records.

My time working with Kevin is a clear demonstration of what I believe to be one of his greatest strengths—his ability to develop people. From the start of our time together back in January 2001, where I served as his interim administrative assistant in the University of Notre Dame Athletic Department, Kevin created an environment where I could learn and grow, providing me with opportunities to learn the business from a front row seat in his office. At that time, as a young professional, fresh out of college, I was truly unsure of my desired career path. I knew "sports" was the industry for me, but I hadn't yet found the specific path/direction within "sports" that ignited a passion for me. Kevin recognized my uncertainty and, instead of pushing me toward a predetermined path, he encouraged exploration and growth. In the six months that I worked in his office, he intentionally, but not forcefully, exposed me to as many aspects of athletic administration as possible.

After obtaining my Juris Doctorate from Tulane Law School and spending three years away from Notre Dame, I found myself drawn back to my alma mater and the opportunity to once again work under Kevin's leadership in the athletic department. Working at Notre Dame in the athletics compliance office allowed me to apply the legal skills I'd honed at Tulane in a real-world athletic environment. Returning to a Dr. White-led program felt like coming home. He had an uncanny ability to create a sense of purpose and camaraderie within the department, making everyone—student-athletes, coaches, administrators, support staff—feel like an integral part of something bigger. Kevin had a way of blending high expectations with genuine support, pushing those around him to excel while ensuring they never felt alone in their pursuit of excellence.

My time at Notre Dame was a dynamic and fulfilling experience, but after three short years, life took me in another exciting direction—Kevin accepted the role of Vice President and Director of Athletics at Duke University. I, along with two other colleagues, had the privilege of accompanying Kevin to work at Duke. The transition to Duke opened up new challenges and opportunities, but one constant remained: Kevin's mentorship, which continued to shape my career in profound ways.

For thirteen years, I worked closely with Kevin, both as his Chief of Staff and Senior Deputy Director of Athletics. I had a front row seat to his decision-making process, his management of a high-profile department, and his ability to navigate complex environments. This exposure was invaluable, allowing me to absorb daily (really, hourly!) lessons on leadership, strategy, and the importance of integrity in athletic administration. I grew into my role at Duke and over the years took on significant responsibilities. Rather than micromanaging, Kevin empowered me, as he did for the entire senior leadership team, he trusted me and guided me as I honed my leadership skills. He believed in me, which without a doubt helped me build confidence and resilience. And one of the best parts was that through all the hard work and long hours, we had fun! Kevin's New York sense of humor made even the most challenging days enjoyable. Whether we were celebrating a big win, tackling a tough decision, or navigating an unexpected curveball, there was often times room for a laugh or a light moment. Kevin had a knack for keeping things in perspective, reminding us all that enjoying the journey mattered just as much as achieving the goals.

During our time at Duke together, my husband Rick and I also developed a deeper personal connection with Kevin and his wife, Jane. They truly embraced us and welcomed us into their family. Jane, with her warmth, genuine kindness, and overall badass attitude, became and still is a dear friend and confidant. She was always there with a listening ear or a word of encouragement, whether it was about the challenges of balancing work and personal life or just sharing stories over a good meal. Her presence added another layer of support and camaraderie to our experience, making our time at Duke feel even more like home. Jane's friendship is something I cherish deeply, and has left an indelible mark on me, Rick, and our sons.

The professional bond that Kevin White and I have reflects a deep trust and respect, and it exemplifies the transformational connection that can form between a mentor and a mentee. Kevin's mentorship gave me the clarity and experience I needed to carve out a fulfilling career in college athletics, eventually leading me to where I am today. Kevin's approach with me was not an isolated example but was in fact, quite the opposite—I am one of many who have benefitted from Kevin White's overall leadership philosophy.

> **Throughout his career, he focused on building up those around him, creating a legacy of successful leaders, administrators and coaches, who thrived under his mentorship. He has a remarkable talent for recognizing potential and fostering it into success.**

College athletics is an arena where success is earned through relentless effort, and the most valuable lessons are often forged in the face of adversity. Every victory, setback, and challenge shapes not just the outcomes on the field, but the character and resilience of those involved. Yet, as Kevin reminds us in the pages that follow, it is also a world filled with opportunities to make a lasting impact on the lives of individuals. The reflections in this book offer a window into the profound influence that coaches, administrators, and mentors can have in shaping the character and futures of people under their guidance.

As you immerse yourself in these pages, I hope you find inspiration not only in the stories but also in the enduring principles that define a life well-lived in college athletics. I hope you are inspired to embrace these lessons in your own leadership journey. May this book guide you in becoming not just a good leader, but a great one—a leader who exemplifies the very best of what it means to be a good sport.

To me, this book is not just a guide for those in the world of college athletics—it's a blueprint for how to lead with heart, how to face challenges with integrity, and how to inspire others to be their best. I hope that as you read it, you'll feel the same sense of gratitude and admiration that I do for Dr. Kevin White, a man whose impact extends far beyond the pages of this book, for he truly is the "Godfather of College Athletics."

With deep appreciation and respect,

Nina King
Vice President and Director of Athletics/
Adjunct Professor of Business Administration
Duke University

INTRODUCTION

"The best way to predict the future is to create it."

PETER DRUCKER

Mandalay Bay Resort, Las Vegas: June 2022. Sitting at a banquet table covered in a heavy, oversized, white tablecloth on an elevated stage with two colleagues (Jennifer Heppel and Allen Greene), we looked like the head table at a typical wedding reception; yet the overall atmosphere was infused with thoughts of divorce from the institution of collegiate athletics as we knew it.

Jennifer, Allen, and I were invited to speak in a panel discussion at the annual National Association of Collegiate Directors of Athletics (NACDA) Convention, which represents over 21,000 members, to discuss the grave issues facing college sports in America. This session was in one of the larger ballrooms, and it was jam-packed—standing room only. Tom Nevala, a Director for Huron Consulting Group, presided at the podium and asked us a series of pointed questions.

Huron is a management consulting firm that focuses on providing third party review, expert opinions, and business operations strategies/plans to colleges and universities, which now includes the collegiate athletics space as well. They currently represent some 400 colleges and universities and guide them through potential solutions to issues around higher education. In full disclosure, I now work for them as a senior advisor.

One year prior to the NACDA conference, in June of 2021, individual states had already begun rolling out potential NIL (Name, Image, and Likeness) legislation piecemeal, most of which was unsurprisingly permissive without any forethought or understanding of how it might affect the collegiate athletics system. Meanwhile, the NCAA was pushing to pass all-encompassing legislation that included guardrails meant to limit the effect of NIL benefits on the recruiting process, such as direct payments from boosters to student-athletes, etc. Although it was not widely agreed-upon across member institutions, the pressure was on to come up with something that would create a level playing field for both institutions and student-athletes throughout the entire country. When we were unable to make that happen, individual institutions were forced to write their own rules based on whatever laws their home states enacted. However, following the Supreme Court's ruling on *Alston v. NCAA*, which upheld the decision that the NCAA could not restrict student-athlete academic benefits due to antitrust violation, the NCAA opened the door wide for NIL benefits without any real regulation or organization. Changes were slow-moving that first year, but, by the summer of 2022, as institutions started to observe the impacts of the Supreme Court's ruling, it was all anyone could talk about.

As Tom indicated that it was my turn to answer the big question looming over the room, I sat up in my chair with all the freedom of a newly retired player. Speaking from the heart, I ranted on in front of over 500 Athletic

Directors and NCAA staffers regarding how we might save our beloved enterprise from itself. The chaos of college athletics had gone from untenable to toxic.

Accordingly, I gave a rather candid assessment of what was at stake if we did not move to regulate it…and *fast*. I had publicly blasted the concept of NIL (Name, Image, and Likeness) early on, predicting many pejorative outcomes. And yet here we were, stuck with it and scrambling to problem-solve. In short, my commentary was a bold declaration of our collective failure as stewards of one of the most legendary organizations in America. *And yes, I include myself in that failure 100%*. We—all the ADs, commissioners, and select others in the room—are responsible for this train wreck. The NCAA is an association of 1,100 members who dictate what happens; it took a community to make this mess. For years, we had been like the Titanic heading straight into the iceberg. We all saw it coming yet refused to change course. Now, we were living with the consequences of a pay-for-play model, which is a far cry from where we'd been historically. Add to that the transfer portal, which allows players to move freely from school to school based purely on financial gain at the whims of NIL benefactors—and we were facing what I believed to be the beginning of the end of inter-collegiate athletics.

Needless to say, the crowd's reactions to my eulogy were mixed—some thought I went too dark. Yet, I am in daily conversations with those in power to fix it, and at this point—we are all in this together. There are approximately 500,000 active student-athletes representing 1,100 NCAA institutions, and they all want the same thing: a more contemporary financial model for athletes.

The enhanced visibility of athletes across television, social media, etc. has encouraged fans to become more "tribal" than ever before. And of course, this has proven to be an invaluable asset for the broader higher education community. More than 3,000 colleges and universities in America utilize athletics to enhance their position within their well-defined market.

> **Unfortunately, the traditional, over one-hundred-year-old model, wherein college athletics is a validating partner within higher education, is currently at risk.**

There exists a competing interest to further commercialize and/or monetize this enormous dimension of institutional advancement. Thus, this has become an impassioned battle between education and entertainment, a battle in which student-athletes stand to lose the most. In my professional opinion, it is morally and ethically irresponsible to promise the parents of an eighteen to twenty-two-year-old kid that you are going to nurture and guide their most precious gift if you are really just looking at your team roster as a list of game pieces on a Monopoly board.

College athletes are still just young men and women, each navigating their own pathway of personal development, which includes building character, intellect, leadership qualities, loyalty, etc. However, if we continue down this road of "every man/woman for themselves," will all of our most talented athletes miss out on the significant intellectual and emotional growth that can only be fostered within the complete student-athlete experience? And will they not be afforded the opportunity to be guided through adversity by well-intentioned and invested coaches and mentors instead of just jumping into the portal? Will they never learn what it is to be selfless, to play and win for their teammates and their school? Those are life lessons that should continue to resonate for the rest of their lives, making them better human beings and future leaders in society. Does anyone actually believe that these young kids are ready to forego all of the above and just "wing it" as adults who manage themselves?

Yes, we are part of the entertainment business, and there is great opportunity for all parties to benefit financially. But we must not allow that profit to override our primary responsibilities as educators, coaches, and mentors. By not having strict rules and regulations in place when NIL rolled out, we have damaged the student-athlete experience for many young men and women.

****

Merrion Hotel, Dublin: July 2022. A month later, more than twenty former colleagues and close friends surprised Jane and me in Ireland to help us celebrate our retirement from forty-seven years of teaching, coaching, and athletics administration. They knew we were in Dublin for our Fiftieth Wedding Anniversary and that our kids and grandkids would be arriving the following week. These incomparable men and women had survived in the trenches with us at athletic departments across America throughout the past four decades, serving at Loras College, University of Maine, Tulane University, Arizona State University, University of Notre Dame, and Duke University. We had a hell of a party with some much-needed craic on none other than the greatest island on earth.

> **Within college athletics, beyond resource acquisition, we also find ourselves in the leadership acquisition and development business—a reality that we must acknowledge and openly embrace.**

Well over thirty of my former staffers have become Directors of Athletics, Conference Commissioners, and/or pinnacle leaders in just about every dimension of the greater collegiate athletics landscape. To be sure, at the risk of sounding slightly arrogant, our cohort has majored in integrity, transparency, doing the right thing when nobody is watching, treating others the way you'd want to be treated, and being authentic as hell. Moreover, we have placed a serious premium on my great friend General Martin Dempsey's motto, "make it matter!"

However, the dialogue in Dublin was also fueled by enormous concern, as depicted in Las Vegas. Since then, I have been engaged in daily communication with most of the leaders within the industry, if not participating on respective podcasts, or providing zoom talks around the dramatic changes facing college athletics—mostly concerning the unsustainable, financial hemorrhaging, "pay for play" NIL model. There are now endless, ongoing forums where this dialogue is being fully digested. American higher education was built on an equalitarianism mentality. Freshman composition pays for metaphysics not unlike football and men's basketball supply the resources for all other Olympic sports. The university concept, historically, has been designed to be universal, holistically satisfying the needs and interests of the eclectic student body. This will undoubtedly be a supreme challenge moving forward!

****

Durham, North Carolina: March 2023. At the very core of my journey from Amityville, NY to Durham, NC, is the nonnegotiable theory that we are all products of our own environment (and select experiences), which is closely aligned with our DNA, or forebearers if you will.

> **All success begins when one taps into their instinctive ambition and resilience.**

Growing up in an enormously proud second-generation Irish American family in 1960s New York as the oldest of four children with parents who had no formal high school or college education, gave me a sense of urgency to hustle a dollar without any hesitation, which quickly developed my business acumen. Resource acquisition, or what I like to call the "loaves and fishes" game, has perhaps defined my professional longevity, if not my legacy.

Today, college sports are inarguably a major piece of the economic engine that exists within the larger, global sporting portfolio. More precisely, according to an economic analysis of sport back in 2015, it was calculated that domestic sport in total represented 6.1% of the GDP (Gross Domestic Product), or $985B within the U.S. economy. Conversely, global sport represented roughly 4.7% of the world economy, or $3T. Given that, it would be easy to make the case that sport has become "pop culture" at a minimum, and thus it has been deemed highly influential in terms of corporate marketing, and/or basic individual association, if not identity.

There is little debate that the NFL and the NBA are the supreme catalysts relative to driving the sports business machinery. However, considering broadcast property contracts and many other sources of revenue, college sports have also become a very sizable piece of the economic engine, no longer far behind the high-profile professional sport segment of the entertainment market.

The NCAA has appointed a new leader: Charlie Baker, former Governor of Massachusetts; he is a highly successful businessman and politician with no prior experience in the world of college athletics. NCAA President Baker is facing a sharp learning curve as he endeavors to chart the course forward and maintain the traditional exploits of the modern era of college sports, while building on the contemporary movement, which has become a stunning reality over the past decade as the NCAA membership has adopted a more permissive mindset.

That said, at the crux of the immediate dilemma is the potential advent of the redistribution of existing resources. If you subscribe to the theory that the resource base is pretty well defined, then any redistribution will result in "winners and losers." My concern is that, as permissiveness grows, those redirected resources will be at the expense of the NCAA Olympic sports and/or the Olympic Movement more broadly. The NCAA has become the training ground for Team USA; 80% of Team USA, as well as 40% of the Paralympic Team emanates from our NCAA system.

The distinct marriage of college sport and higher education only exists in the United States. No other countries enjoy this highly distinctive model, although Western Europe and Asia have seriously studied just how they might emulate this partnership. Ironically, higher education in America is a direct reflection of Western Europe, and at this moment, there exists considerable European interest in emulating the school and sport model, relative to institutional branding, philanthropy, enhanced connectivity to all constituencies, and so on.

For almost a half a century, my keen interests have been at the intersection of school and sport, centered around the relationship between education and entertainment, particularly within the college athletics space.

> **In all humility, I am the only practitioner in the business who has been a high school and college track coach as well as a director of athletics at Notre Dame and Duke. Along the way, I have served in leadership roles at a range of public and private colleges and universities.**

This adaptability underscores my unique upbringing as well as my long career to date.

As I write this, American higher education is in a tug-of-war; the trending corporate environment wages a significant, if not dramatic, makeover.

> **Given the targeted challenges of the day, this unfiltered manuscript allows the reader to become more familiar with the politicization of college sport—which is inarguably the most political element within higher education—and to understand the dynamics surrounding college athletics administration at a terribly chaotic moment in its glorious history.**

In my attempt to guide readers through the complex and at times illusive facets of leadership and politics based on my life experience, I will be blending the personal and the professional, just like life. The plan is to take the reader behind the curtain to provide earnest insight relative to the ringmaster, to provide backstage access to the circus across a spectrum of institutions, and to offer some crystal-ball analysis relative to the future realities of the greater enterprise moving forward.

My sincere hope is to not only unveil the inner workings of athletics administration and coaching, but to negate the idea that the only roadmap to a productive life is emanating from the right bassinet.

> **As I walk you through my forty-seven-year career, and account for the select knowledge acquired along the way, my hope is that you will further embrace your own existence and envision your own pathway to your destination of choice.**

As they say, not all roads lead to Chicago. Sometimes, an alternate route can deliver you to an exotic destination that is most compatible with your dream. Clearly, I don't believe that there is any one set path to success, so while some of my stories may initially appear not to be heading anywhere, my yesteryear reflections are in fact key signs on the road ahead.

So, whether you are just along for the ride, whether you share my passion for athletics, or whether you are looking for a map to climb the proverbial life ladder via collegiate sport—get on the bus, you made the travel squad!

CHAPTER 1

IRISH ANCESTRY: INSPIRATION

> "The best journeys answer questions that in the beginning you didn't even think to ask"
>
> JEFF JOHNSON, *180° SOUTH*

As I examine the triggers within my life that have motivated and prepared me for my professional vocation as a servant leader, July of 2022 marks a massive moment of introspection. For well over two years, my wife Jane had been planning an amazing family trip to Ireland, originally meant to commemorate our fiftieth wedding anniversary. Of course, when I concluded my vice president and director of athletics duties at Duke University in June 2021, a retirement party was waved off due to the COVID-19 shut-down. Hence, our whole family agreed to meet in Ireland during the summer of 2022 to celebrate both our fiftieth anniversary and my semi-official retirement.

Jane and I flew into Dublin, then drove 250 miles northwest to my ancestral home up in Dungloe, County Donegal. The rest of the family was scheduled to arrive a week later, which provided us with ample time to visit both of our families' homesteads—in Roshine South and Falmore, respectively.

Navigating the winding roads, with endless rotaries, up to Dungloe, I found myself reflecting on the summer of 1963 when I took part in the pre-seminary program with the Graymoor Friars up in Montour Falls, New York. As a young boy within a classic Irish Catholic family, when the pastor comes to your home and tells both your parents and immigrant grandparents that he thinks you have a holy vocation, you are not a part of the decision-making process. Once Father Fuchs made that proclamation, it was a foregone conclusion. Within our home, as well as in all the homes of my extended family, there were many portraits depicting the honorable and beloved Monsignor Hugh O'Donnell, my mother's cousin. This provided serious implied pressure, to be sure. Given that, before I could renegotiate my fate, I found myself on a bus to upstate New York with forty-five other pre-seminarian prospects.

Instantly, upon being treated to an overdose of tranquility and prayer, I recognized that I was squarely out of my element. Most days, we would be in chapel, while I was totally consumed with the great outdoors, peering at the ball fields, hoping to be allowed to escape a prayer session. Near the end of the summer, just before the group was going to be sent home prior to commencing seminary high school in a few short weeks, we were all gathered in the cafeteria. A resident friar conveyed the details of our break, highlighting the start of high school matriculation, and then transitioned to, "If any of you are not sure that you want this life, I'll be in my office after dinner." Immediately, I dropped my fork to ensure that I would be first in line, which I was, whereby I most respectfully delivered the "I am out of here" message. The priest indicated that he understood and offered to drive me back downstate the next day.

Jane and Kevin 1993 Ireland Trip

About three hours or so into our drive, the priest asked if I was hungry. Of course, I jumped at that invitation. He then asked if a Howard Johnson's might be appealing, and I quickly let him know that any food was appealing to me. As we pulled off the interstate, it was clear that this Ho Jo was jam-packed—customers were standing in line out the door. The priest pressed forward to speak with the hostess, and my impression was that he was most confident that he would be provided a table in short order. No sooner than the hostess suggested that it might be a forty-five-minute wait, a handsome man in a gray flannel suit stood up and waved us over to his table.

The man kindly invited the good father and the kid (me) to join him for lunch. With little delay, the gentleman asked about the nature of our travel. The priest, who had been trying to re-recruit me all morning, indicated that I had been attending the Graymoor Friar pre-seminary program; he had to explain that this young man (me) thought he wanted to become a priest but has now pivoted. The gentleman jumped in and said something like,

A painting of Kevin's family and ancestral homestead in Dungloe, County Donegal, Ireland

"Perhaps God has yet another plan for this young man. Not to worry, these things tend to work out for the best." Then, in a heroic effort to stop my berating, he shared that he was a product of parochial education, and that he attended the University of Notre Dame. His name was none other than Jim Crowley, one of the legendary "Four Horsemen." The priest, not unlike me, almost ate his fork. In 2000, when I was introduced as the director of athletics at Notre Dame, I seriously wondered if Jim Crowley was looking down, and whether he'd remember our prophetic meeting.

Having made the road trip from Dublin to Donegal annually for the past thirty years, I knew exactly how little was left of the drive. Every year since 1993, Jane and I have visited my ancestral home in Dungloe, County Donegal, Ireland, where my maternal grandparents emigrated from 100 years ago. Finally, the road opened to reveal picturesque Falmore—a twenty-eight-home, back-in-time, residential community within greater Dungloe, overlooking the mighty Atlantic.

The family homestead was built by James Boyle, my great-great grandfather, and it is currently owned by Jack and Martin Brereton. Upon arrival, we had breakfast with Jack and Martin, who have resided in the home for many years now. Their seven-acre property also houses the ruins where my grandmother, Mariah Boyle O'Donnell, was born and raised. In Roshine South, about four miles from Falmore, sits the O'Donnell (Hugh O'Donnell) homestead, which is where my grandfather, Patrick O'Donnell, was born and raised in a sublet called Roshine Bay. The lure of the endless pristine landscape, unobstructed views, and wildflowers which inhabit the unencumbered terrain of an elevated mountain ridge while the sea beckons below is only compounded by our rich family history.

Kevin's Maternal Grandparents from Dungloe - seated Mary(Mariah) and Patrick.

> **Although I cannot claim direct residency, Dungloe is my North Star.**

These family trips to Ireland were partially instigated by my Uncle, Jimmy "Spot" O'Donnell. I fondly remember how proud he was to take his immediate family to Ireland, and how, as a young man, I was enthralled by their stories. In fact, it was my Uncle Jimmy who facilitated our first trip to the island back in 1993.

Back in the '80s, my Uncle Jimmy and Aunt Mary annually hosted Irish educators at their residence in Harvey's Lake, Pennsylvania, while the teachers completed graduate work at King's College in nearby Wilkes Barre. In the early '90s, they hosted a man by the name of Des Broderick, a professor from St. Patrick's College in Maynooth, Ireland (a sublet of Dublin). At the time, Jane and I lived in Louisiana while I was the AD at Tulane University. Prof. Broderick was interested in visiting both Tulane and New Orleans, so Uncle Jimmy encouraged him to contact me.

The following summer, Des and his wife, Kay came to stay at our home. And throughout his week-long visit, we became good friends. In turn, a year or so later, Des formally invited Jane and me to provide a consultancy around college athletics at St. Patrick's College in Dublin. At the time, there was no connection within Irish higher education between school and sport. In addition, the administration expressed an ardent desire to launch a philanthropy program—back then, St. Patrick's was governmentally (federally) supported, and fundraising was not yet a part of the institution's financial equation. This was all very much in my wheelhouse, so we readily agreed. Fast forward to today—St. Patrick's has become a leader in Irish higher education, offering a collegiate athletics experience which emulates the American model. Furthermore, institutional philanthropy across higher education within Ireland had become a reality. The powerful combination of those two elements, not unlike within the states, has proven to be a pivotal conduit to alumni, benefactors, the public at large, and a growing institutional brand.

Ironically, St. Patrick's had a distinctive Catholic private school vibe. Not surprising, for it was founded as a seminary before pivoting to an educationally focused curriculum. Moreover, the top three officers of the college were Catholic priests. Two home-grown Irishmen, one of which graduated from Georgetown, and the other from Boston College. The third priest was a native New Yorker who graduated from Fordham.

Over the course of our first stay in Maynooth, conversation surrounding our Irish ancestral roots emanated and became a topic of supreme interest between myself and our Irish hosts. I conveyed to our friends that, although I was proudly the first high school graduate within our immediate family, we were related to two teachers who taught in County Donegal prior to their emigration. They were called Daniel and James. The priests quickly asserted that if they were credentialed teachers, they would have attended St. Patrick's—for it was the only option for certification at the time of their work. Amazingly, when we met for breakfast the next morning, the good fathers handed us copies of both Daniel and James's college transcripts, which appeared to have been recorded by a No. 2 pencil.

Toward the end of our visit, Prof. Broderick insisted on driving us up to Dungloe. We eagerly contacted Wee Hughie O'Donnell, a cousin, who expressed utter delight at our prospective visit. When we arrived, Wee Hughie offered us a drink of Hennessy whiskey. Following the libation, he began showing us around town and leading us to the family homesteads. In one very telling exchange, he pointedly asked what we did for a living. I told Wee Hughie that I worked in college athletics in New Orleans, Louisiana, at Tulane University—none of which was really understood. Then, Wee Hughie treated us to some fascinating stories about our family's connection, if not leadership, within the Invincibles, Molly Maguire's, and eventually the IRA—for Dungloe is quite close to the Northern Ireland border. In fact, one of the teachers noted earlier, Daniel O'Donnell, was captured during the Rising and then incarcerated in Dublin until his eventual prison break, before landing in New Jersey, as a lifelong educator under an alias.

Throughout my childhood, many of our extended Irish family members came to visit our home in New York or Uncle Jimmy's home in Pennsylvania. So, I asked Wee Hughie, "Why didn't you ever come over for a visit?"

He firmly responded, "Oh, that Goddamn New York! I'd never go there." And when I rationed that Dublin was pretty cosmopolitan, not unlike a smaller New York, Wee Hughie was quick to add: "I'd never go to Dublin either!"

In 1998, five years after our first meeting, I visited Wee Hughie in a very "near the end" scene at the local Dungloe hospital. He was on his way out, and I was essentially visiting him to say goodbye. Incoherently, he said to me, "You said you'd come back, but you never did!" Obviously, he was confusing me with another, perhaps even expired, family member. When asked what I could do for him, he gently asked me to sneak him in another pint of Hennessy, for his concealed allotment was running low. My thoughts were mired in childhood memories of my grandmother, Mariah, with whom I shared a room during her extended stays on Franklin St. in Amityville. She'd walk into my closet each night before bed, take down her little bottle of whiskey from the top shelf and take a big swig under the glow of the closet light. Then she'd simply stow it back behind the sweaters and hop into her bed. Back then, although we were proud to be of Irish decent, our family worked extremely hard to assimilate into mainstream America.

> **When our grandparents stayed with us on Long Island, tales of Dungloe would permeate our South Shore existence, igniting in me a profound interest in precisely where we emanated from, for we hadn't been in America all that long.**

The White Family - Ireland Trip Summer 2022

After Jane and I said goodbye to Jack and Martin, we left Dungloe and departed for Dublin with a sense of gratitude and grounding. When we arrived, we met the rest of our family. All twenty-five of us—including my five children, their respective spouses, and thirteen of sixteen grandkids (three little ones did not make the travel squad)—happily executed the Jane White family travel agenda all over Ireland! Circuitously, we traveled around Dublin, toured St. Patrick's Cathedral, visited the Burren, kayaked and paddle-boarded in Galway Bay, and took in the Cliffs of Moher and the Aran Islands. The entire crew also spent several hours at the Irish American Museum down in New Ross, where we experienced a reenactment of the harrowing crossings so many Irish families braved during the Potato Famine via a recreated ship, the Dunbrody. The talented actors on the ship were masterful in their ability to convey the hardships of the famine period in Irish history. Each family member, youngest to oldest, was deeply touched by the experience—a part of our shared history made real.

With a sharpened sense of appreciation, and far more blessings than any of us deserve, we traveled on to Lahinch and Doolin (where we made a steady diet of O'Connor's Pub). All of our immigrant relatives, especially my maternal grandparents—Patrick O'Donnell and Mariah Boyle—were indeed celebrated!

Mary ("Mariah") O'Donnell, an accomplished Irish step-dancer, was a maid and a nanny upon weathering the elongated onboarding and employment-finding process following her arrival at Ellis Island in 1907. Patrick O'Donnell, who arrived at Ellis Island somewhat under protest, had been a horse trainer in Roshine South. When they arrived in Brooklyn, there were absolutely no horse training positions available. So, my grandfather began working as a laborer in a Pittsburgh steel mill, then pivoted to an eastern Pennsylvania coal mine to be among a large cohort of Donegal immigrants in Wilkes Barre where they raised three children: my Aunt Aileen, my Uncle Jimmy, and my mother Rita.

Patrick came to be known as Black Paddy after he was burned badly in a coal mine fire which prematurely upended his work life. He would not have had any workman's comp, proper healthcare, or insurance in that era, so his burns were not treated properly. The skin on his left arm was like a melted candle, and his fingers healed by growing together. Of course, there was little need for a maid or nanny when they settled in a lower working-class Wilkes Barre, Pennsylvania enclave. Therefore, my grandmother taught Irish step-dancing in the apartments they rented, whereby her highly skilled students would be afforded at least an opportunity to be sent to a convent in the Bronx, with the promise of a Roxyette (precursor to the NYC

Rockettes) tryout. Mariah's apartment dance lessons were arranged via the barter system, in exchange for a can of soup or a few potatoes.

For Mariah and Patrick O'Donnell, this trip represented a long way from getting off that damn ship at Ellis Island with one suitcase in hand, preoccupied with the American dream.

> **To say the least, Ireland has been a mystical place that has fueled our life journey. We have a deep sense of where we came from, as well as a supreme sense of the many debilitating challenges our families had to overcome.**

One of my all-time favorite days was when I was granted dual Irish citizenship. Being formally connected to my Irish legacy, particularly my family heritage in Dungloe, was a powerful moment for me. I am grateful, not only for the opportunities that America has given me, but also for the opportunities my parents and grandparents were given in this country. America is an amazing place that has been greatly enhanced by its eclectic migration and evolution. Our ancestral story is not unique; however, our journey is indeed very personal and will be forever celebrated.

> **Thank God there was no "wall" in those days, for America was immeasurably impacted by immigrants from all corners of the world— including the Irish—whose legacy I strive to uphold as an immensely proud Irish American.**

As for goals, they have remained straightforward; both Jane and I have always been determined to stand on the shoulders of our parents and grandparents, and to be the best versions of ourselves to support our proud family legacy. To be pointed, our supreme goal has been to "cash in" on all the generational hardships endured by our family and to recreate, in the best way possible, the record of our extended family moving forward. Jane and I have upheld the nonnegotiable commitment to provide limitless opportunities for our five children. Today, all five have families of their own, and they have all enjoyed careers in education or athletics. Given all of that, our sixteen grandchildren will soon be given the infamous torch to march up the proverbial mountain of life, not unlike their parents and grandparents.

As I transition to the next segment of the book, let me simply say that the unqualified benefits of having a sense of where you came from, coupled with clearly defined future/ongoing aspirations, can make one feel like they held up a Brinks Truck!

CHAPTER 2

LEARNING HOW TO PLAY THE GAME: THE WILDS OF LONG ISLAND

> "So here I stand…looking at the house we called home for so many years. The man I am now longing to see the world as a child again, when every sight and sound was a marvel. I can see myself, a ghost boy…"
>
> GABRIEL BYRNE, *WALKING WITH GHOSTS*

As I relaunch the currach, and paddle my way into chapter two, the bright lights of New York shine on my family. My mother, Rita O'Donnell, was just fifteen years old and a sophomore at Coughlin High School in 1940 when her older sister (my aunt), Aileen O'Donnell Marlowe urged her to quit school and move to New York City. As they say, the rest is history…

Rita, following her big sister, began her NYC dancing career which would last for ten years. The sisters moved into a convent in the Bronx, viewing this as the best way to escape their coal-mining community. There they vowed to stay until they could comfortably support themselves as dancers via their mother's training. Mariah had trained the girls well, and it didn't take long for them to find success. They both danced with the Roxyettes and then the New York City Rockettes. In addition to performing in countless shows throughout the city, they entertained the U.S. troops during WWII on USO Tours alongside the likes of Bob Hope. My Aunt Aileen became a sister-in-law to Jannette McDonald and Gene Raymond, appeared in seven motion pictures, and later served as the head choreographer for Jerry Lewis Productions for twenty-five years. My mother, Rita, became a plus-one duet singing partner with significant crooners of the late 40s such as Bing Crosby, Frank Sinatra, and Danny Kaye, just to name a few. Frank Sinatra, the legend himself, fondly referred to her as "the little coal cracker."

Kevin's mother, Rita, and a friend in New York.

Rita's signature "knock 'em dead song" was "Danny Boy." I've been told many times that my mother was pure magic on stage. As the legend goes, there was not a breath in the room while she sang. I can tell you that many times over the years, she was equally as magical in our living room. We would all goad her to sing "Danny Boy" at parties, and I would look around and watch people—who had never even heard the song before—be transported by her voice and just tear up. Many family members have tried to channel Rita in this regard, me included. However, we've all failed miserably.

In Rita's heyday, she was on the cover of Cue Magazine in 1946 and 1949 as the "Chesterfield (a popular cigarette brand) Woman of the Year." (Ironically, in 1998, she passed away after a horrific battle with COPD.) While she remained a relatively obscure show girl, Rita always had work. On one such gig, she connected with a stagehand who espoused to someday become a successful song writer and performer in his own right. Rita was sixteen at the time, and the stagehand, Mel Torme, was seventeen. He ended up writing "The Christmas Song" (*Chestnuts roasting on an open fire...*) as a gift for Rita, who proudly claimed that she was the first to sing the song accompanied by Mel at his piano. The song was released in 1946. Nonetheless, the couple did not last, and, as fate would have it, Rita married Emerson White in 1949.

Kevin's mother, Rita, at the back stage door of the Roxy Theater.

On the White side of the family ledger, both of my father's parents were abandoned orphans in New York City, and they spent most of their adult life together in Brooklyn. However, my own DNA is 97% Celtic (mostly Irish, with no other ethnicity registered) and Reuben (Pop to me) White did have a birth certificate which said that his mother (an O'Donnell if you can believe it) died at birth. My paternal grandmother, Catherine White, known as Kitty, was a cook at the Brooklyn Navy Yard. She was everyone's favorite within their six-floor walkup, for she supplied the entire building with leftovers from her cafeteria. As for Pop White, he was a failed vaudevillian—a soft-shoe dance man with a straw hat and cane. Once he was disinvited from the vaudeville scene, he became a billboard painter in Manhattan, prior to landing the position as building superintendent at every one of the apartment buildings in which the family lived over the next several decades.

Together, Reuben and Kitty raised three children in these colorful Brooklyn communities: my father, Emerson White, my Aunt Annabelle, and my Uncle Eddy. As a teenager, my father forged a close friendship with the yet to become famous sitcom actor, Jackie Gleason. Their particular six-floor walkup actually became the backdrop of America's first sitcom, *The Honeymooners*! All of the families in residence, as well as their sir names, were utilized by Jackie as he created this wildly popular comedy. Truth be told, I was often dropped off at this storied building in Ridgewood, Brooklyn to be looked after by these infamous sitcom characters while my parents visited Manhattan for the day. As I watch reruns today, I still smirk.

My father, Emerson James White, attended high school until grade eleven, and was a voracious reader and self-directed intellect. Having been born the eldest child of two orphaned parents who worked diligently to climb from utter poverty to lower middle class, Emmy always wanted more. He had big plans—dreams aplenty of a middle-class existence not unlike the ones he had seen portrayed in the early days of sitcom television, where the American Dream was portrayed nearly every night. Of course, for Emmy, he must have felt like he hit the ball out of the park when he married a dancer and big band singer. As the story goes, he met Rita one night at the stage door after one of her shows in New York City.

Emmy was a leader among his contemporaries and started several choruses via the Society for the Preservation and Encouragement of Barbershop Singing in America (SPEBSA), which performed around New York. Moreover, he facilitated a few large-scale productions, in which my mother also performed.

> **Sports and entertainment are unmistakably linked in this country, and when I think of my parents, I see where my big dreams, enterprising ideas, and unrelenting ambition come from.**

In the late 1950s, my father met Mr. James Clark, an officer from First National City Bank on Manhattan's Park Avenue. The two met through a barbershop chorus connection. Clark had been charged with finding a street salesman that could successfully launch a new banking product in Staten Island. Before credit cards as we know them existed, this product was called the "Everything Card," and it required my dad to sell the local butcher, pharmacist, haberdasher, etc., on the concept of this new payment method and get them to come on board with utilizing it in their businesses. They imagined that a broad network, in terms of purchasing across different retail platforms and outlets, could be incorporated. Hence, First National City Bank hired Emmy White, and they encouraged him to amass a sales force. So, my dad hired six St. John's University grads (he forever loved St. John's) and hit the streets of Staten Island with his pilot endeavor. The "Everything Card" eventually morphed into the Bank Americard, then Visa, and so on. My dad loved his job, but just like most of his exciting professional endeavors, there was a defined shelf-life.

From there, with an enormous appetite for sports and the entertainment business, he began writing a free trivia column that was distributed in local shopping districts all across Long Island. It became a popular, weekly syndicated column depicting the goings on in both of his favorite topics. His column was published in all or most of the local Long Island newspapers, as well as a few others in and around New York City. Although this was a labor of love, it couldn't be monetized.

After serious droughts of unemployment, he jumped into selling cars before finally, in the '70s, opening a bar alongside a few acquaintances. At the risk of sounding cynical, Emmy was the partner with the clean record, for alcohol licenses are most difficult to obtain in New York. The "Ole Straw Hat" was a play-off of my mother and grandfather's stage careers. The concept was to create a meeting place fashioned after the traditional neighborhood Irish Pub. Coupled with entertainment and some karaoke, the pub's ultimate intent was to recruit performers who had recently appeared on Ed Sullivan or the like. The founders hoped to attract folks to Amityville for late-night sets after their high-profile Manhattan engagements had ended. This was an odd business undertaking for a non-drinker. However, Emmy loved a good song and/or standup set. He especially loved seeing my mother and her dear friend, Carol Ryan, rock the place! Incidentally, Rita White and Carol Ryan mirrored my dad's advancement of the Society for the Preservation and Encouragement of Barbershop Singing in America by promoting, like crazy, the Sweet Adeline's (a female chorus group) across Long Island. Both of my parents loved to entertain!

Without any formal schooling, I always struggled to discern just how in the hell my father was so damn smart! Emerson somehow knew just where everyone's buttons were located; and he knew precisely how and when to push the right one. Moreover, he exuded a masculine odor of sorts, and his nicotine-stained orange fingers made him, by anyone's measure, memorable. No joke, if I close my eyes, I can easily conjure up a stiff remembrance of his defining aroma. Emmy was incredibly well read and could charm the bark off a tree with a soft-sell technique that proved to be inordinately successful in all personal relationships. He was always the supreme leader, the group facilitator, and the guy around whom folks enjoyed spending quality time.

Most unfortunately, perhaps because of his lack of formal education/credentials, although a world-class dreamer, and someone who could honestly come up with an entrepreneurial idea a minute—he never really got out of the blocks in terms of securing sustainable employment.

There were moments when my parents approached the door to middle class, only to suffer yet another dramatic setback. The prospect of potential car repossession and home foreclosure were a mainstay, as was the personal humiliation of having holiday meals delivered to our door by people I knew from school or church. At times, I became an "adolescent coach," strongly encouraging my beloved father to regain his strength and confidence to re-enter the real world—to compete for a piece of the damn pie. Other times, it caused me to quasi-exit a traditional high school experience, because even the income I generated off the bench as a teen had a modest impact.

Without knowing it at the time, my father taught me to be enormously resilient, to mask my insecurities and vulnerabilities to outsiders, and to simply find my way. There is little doubt that I attained my ability to lead throughout my life due to my father's informal training. He was an extremely caring individual, sometimes to a fault, inordinately empathetic, and knew how to lead others (including myself and my siblings) toward significant achievement.

Leadership theorists often espouse four distinct characteristics of a leader: 1) empathy, 2) task orientation, 3) the ability to be flexible, adaptable, and situational, and 4) passion and intensity. Providentially, I was blessed to be raised by parents who embodied all of the above, even though they did not have the educational or career opportunities to capitalize on their innate leadership lottery tickets.

> **Empathy is the most significant characteristic of a leader; it is not a science that can be taught, but truly an art form. The ability to know exactly who someone is and where they are in life, and to be able to place yourself in their given position is priceless.**

Therefore, a high degree of authentic empathy is critical to leadership, and my father was a master in that regard. Emerson (Emmy) White was a big dreamer and natural influencer; he had the power to make anyone feel like they could achieve anything in life. An effective leader will enable an individual or group to do something they wouldn't otherwise accomplish. Emmy had this knack for seeing the best in people and bringing it out; he naturally inspired loyalty by building people up and encouraging them to do things that they never thought they could do. Emmy White has most profoundly influenced my leadership style and the way I view people in general; his observable behavior was highly impactful in my own development. If I've had half the impact on athletes that I've coached or coaches and administrators that I've mentored as my father had on me—that will be my greatest contribution to the industry.

When I was about ten years old, I found myself sitting in the kitchen at my Aunt Mary and Uncle Jimmy's house on Laurel Street in Wilkes Barre, PA. My siblings, cousins, and I were eating scrambled eggs and toast for dinner. My grandmother presided over the dinner detail. As I was engulfed in my evening food allotment, Nanny O'Donnell showed up at the table with a perfectly prepared cheeseburger and a plate of hand-cut french-fries—this looked to me like a Norman Rockwell painting of America at dinner. Of course, I quickly surmised that this late dinner entree was not intended for me or any of the other kids. Nanny O proclaimed that she had prepared this terribly appetizing meal for Uncle Jimmy because he was heading to WORK (the night shift), which warranted *real* food. To be sure, it was at that moment that I came to understand what it meant to earn. "Work" became my mantra.

That said, I always had a bunch of income-generating ideas as a kid. Beyond the traditional snow shoveling and lawn mowing opportunities, I learned how to wax floors and shampoo rugs, eventually purchasing my own equipment before I was twelve. Given that, a family friend with a commercial rug cleaning business began driving me from Long Island to the Winged Foot Golf Club in Mamaroneck, New York. He would drop me off at around 11:00 p.m. and return to pick me up at 6:00 a.m. the next morning, whereby I would shampoo all the rugs for $100 a night from the close of the men's grill until breakfast time. That was pretty good cash for a snot-nosed kid, particularly in 1963! Years later, in college, I would take on late-night rug shampooing jobs for extra cash as well. Early on, I learned a lot about the free-market system.

Necessity taught me how to earn a buck, how to hold my own, and how to compete in an imperfect world.

Life's many imperfections were clearly demonstrated growing up with my maternal, immigrant grandparents who frequently lived with us. Both were from Dungloe, Donegal, Ireland, and they struggled to adapt to their challenging new life in America, albeit equipped with their delightful Donegal brogue. They came from a place where up to 30% of the local economy was made up of funds sent home by family members who uprooted themselves to work in other parts of the world, including the United States. Post Famine, resources in Ireland were so lacking, and money was so desperately needed that around one out of every three family members from Donegal emigrated. My grandfather, Patrick O'Donnell, was met with vehement anti-Irish sentiments such as: "No Irish Need Apply" and "No Mick's for hire!" Not quite the reception he imagined in America. The stories of my grandparents and other family members about the difficulties they faced while finding their way in the world struck a deep-rooted chord within me as a kid, and though the Irish are hardly an underrepresented population today, it homed in me a desire to support the underrepresented populations in and around the college athletics space throughout my career. My keen, unabashed interest in DEI (Diversity, Equity, and Inclusion), if not pluralism, has been developed in absolute earnest.

As I look back, moving to 16 Franklin St. in Amityville, New York, gave our family a home base and provided a discernible pathway forward. Our 1,600-square-foot house with one bathroom had a daily workout, for there were as many as nine or more inhabitants "in play" most of the time. That said, our family was a prototypical 1960s clan. Amityville is the place I continue to call home even at seventy-four years old, and there were a lot of life and business lessons learned there as a kid.

I'll never forget how we managed to get that house. On a random Saturday morning, having just completed third grade at Seaford Manor, my dad said he was taking me for a car ride to Amityville, where we were going to try to buy a house. Apparently, my parents had already been eyeing 16 Franklin St. The seller was a widower, an older gentleman. The list price was $8.5K, supposedly firm. My dad, with his kid in hand, was prepared to offer $8K. However, without employment, obtaining a mortgage was a non-starter. Consequently, my father was hoping this gentleman would hold the mortgage (as in, provide a land contract agreement). Emmy had me take part in a well-defined, choreographed role in the negotiation. He conditioned me to convey that I loved fishing, clamming, and crabbing. And of course, I came out of my shoes to convince the seller. Not to say that I was overly coached, but we were desperate.

The seller told me how his kids grew up on the Great South Bay—for there was a canal just a block away. He was a truly kind individual—exceedingly curious about me and my siblings who would be the immediate beneficiaries of the sale. Even at that tender, naive, age—I gave no evidence that what he described excited the hell out of me; I acted like that world was what I was used to. The gentleman wanted to hear that I would become one with the Great South Bay, and I did. Truth be told, that all somehow became my childhood reality. Growing up, I was terribly enamored with the bay and all of the wonderment and magic it regularly presented. I was infatuated with surfing, boating, and all other water related activities. Salt water everything became my childhood and early adolescent life!

Almost immediately, I felt a part of the historic South Shore community. As a teenager, I enjoyed a serious love affair with surfing, and I spent a fair amount of time at Gilgo Beach, Hemlock Cove, and Ditch Plains in Montauk. The sport symbolized no barriers for me—an equal access reality that inspired an alignment with the natural environment. Even as an adult, my surfing pursuits would take me to Hawaii, Maine, North Carolina, Florida, as well as many locations within California.

Kevin surfing.

Around the age of twelve, while pumping gas and renting rowboats at Buddy Toomey's Boatyard over summer vacation, I proudly used my savings to purchase my very first, very tired, soon-to-be-replaced, lap-streaked wooden rowboat at $4.00 a week over ten weeks, totaling $40. The signed purchase agreement was kept safely within the boatyard cash drawer.

Men often gathered at Buddy Toomey's to consume beer, work on their boats, and trade fishing stories. As I was hosing off the walkway one afternoon, one of these patrons looked deep into the canal and unearthed a five-horsepower Elgin outboard motor that had been underwater for who knows how long. Very dutifully, I took the motor apart, cleaned out the salt residue, and somehow got it running. Thus, I now had a fourteen-foot, old, worn-thin rowboat equipped with a five-horsepower Elgin motor, minus the salt water.

Weeks later, toward the end of the summer of '63, a police officer from Brooklyn came to rent a rowboat for the day to fish in the Great South Bay. When he returned to the dock, aghast by an all-day rowing workout, he asked, "If I come back here, could I rent a motorboat?" Of course, then the conversation segued into "Are there any boats for sale?" Immediately, I sold my custom boat with motor to my newfound friend who offered me $100 on the spot!

Apparently, that night, over a few Schaefers inside Toomey's Bar, the officer had been a bit braggadocious—telling the other patrons how he had hoodwinked the kid on the dock and pretty much stolen a boat with a motor. However, the next morning, on his first voyage, the motor quit. Later that afternoon, the officer, drenched in sweat, showed up at the front door of 16 Franklin Street, demanding a refund. Most unfortunately, his $100 had already been invested in a large grocery haul.

By thirteen, I was buying and selling cars and boats like crazy. The cars were typically not running, and most of my inventory could be characterized as "rescue projects" of little to no value. 16 Franklin Street had a long, thin yard (about 225-feet deep and fifty-feet wide) with an original detached barn-like garage. Within the barn, any boat or car was indeed fixable and marketable. It was not unusual to have an inventory of several cars and maybe a boat or two in the lineup. The Suffolk County Tax office contacted my mother to inquire whether we had filed the appropriate license/paperwork to conduct this ongoing business. Understandably, our neighbors had, at that point, lost their sense of humor. But someone always managed to surface and purchase one of my unsellable items.

In addition to the junkyard marketplace I was running in our yard, we had a dirt driveway. Both my mother and my Irish grandmother were at their wits-end trying to keep up with the constant tracking of dirt into the house, and they would go ballistic when it rained—for the driveway would turn to mud, making an even bigger mess. So, there was an aggressive "push" to create a paved driveway, but the prospect of cement proved to be terribly expensive. Eventually, my father spoke to my Uncle John Perretti, who owned a thriving construction business. He asked Uncle John if he might consider putting in a concrete driveway, and after much negotiating, Big John agreed to drop off a large shipment of red bricks and a pile of sand right on the street in front of our house. To be sure, it was an intimidating stack of red bricks.

Uncle John's men left us with these instructions: "Level the driveway; apply about one-inch of sand; line up the bricks uniformly on top of the sand; pile sand over the bricks; and sweep the sand into the cracks around each brick." My dad, once again, with his soft-sell Brooklynite charisma, could convince anyone to do anything, and I became his next target. Giving zero advice or assistance, he simply told me to create a driveway with the bricks.

As a fairly capable thirteen-year-old, I was a workforce of one! A fair number of highly articulate family members and neighbors observed the job, but at the end of the day, it was my project—assigned to me by my salesman father. Neighbors were totally aghast that a kid was freelancing the project without any real adult supervision. However, this was not terribly unusual; at our house, it was rather commonplace. Somehow, I developed the plan to begin at the back of the house, placing the bricks carefully over an inch of sand, symmetrically distributed throughout the sixty-foot driveway. Once all the bricks were locked into place, I dutifully swept the remaining sand over the top of the bricks to firm up their permanent placement.

> The lifelong "Emmy White" lesson here, which has stood the test of time, is to delegate the endgame/endpoint; and then, to the degree possible, get out of the way! This has been my mantra with coaches, administrative colleagues, and counterparts for most of my professional life.

Over many decades, while visiting our great friends, Mick and Peg McDonough back in Amityville, I've driven or jogged by my old driveway to revisit my craftsmanship.

During the fall of 1965, my dad created a business plan to start a door-to-door dry-cleaning service. Hence, Shamrock Dry Cleaners instantly became an aspiring new business. Emmy cut an arrangement with a traditional dry-cleaning entity in Deer Park, then began hunting for a vehicle. He landed on a 1949 Willy's Jeep that laid dormant in someone's backyard. The car needed a fuel pump and a paint job at the very least. Upon searching salvage yards, my dad found a replacement fuel pump, and one of his close friends installed it. As for the paint job, my dad bought a can of hunter green paint and a brush, and he instructed me to paint the vehicle with a buddy. He then had magnetic signage made for the Jeep. And just like that, we were in the dry-cleaning business, codified as Shamrock Dry Cleaners.

This meant that I too would be thrown back into the work force. I became my father's sidekick, working with him each day in the Jeep and going door to door. Unfortunately, this was my sophomore year of high school, which I hardly ever attended. However, I occasionally showed up for track practice and I never missed a meet.

The only thing standing between Shamrock Dry Cleaners and success was a customer base, a dry-cleaning facility, a reliable vehicle to facilitate pickup and delivery, and a workforce. It sounds funny, but dreams are too often killed by reality. The challenges faced by Shamrock Dry Cleaners are not entirely unlike the challenges that I have since faced at various colleges and universities. At certain times in certain institutions, resources have been woefully incompatible with the programmatic expectations. More often than not, schools want to cultivate brand enhancement coupled with all the incremental institutional advancement benefits of athletics, yet they are reluctant to implement all of the necessary assets and/or infrastructure required to finish the job. Back in the days of Shamrock Dry Cleaners, we were painfully naïve—not to mention misguided—in that specific enterprise.

Even after all these crazy moves and life experiences, I am indeed an "Amityville Guy" at heart; former home of Judy Garland, Will Rogers, Walter O'Malley (Brooklyn Dodgers), and so many others. It's no surprise that our family, with deep show business roots would "kill" to be associated with this yesteryear summer paradise relative to the Manhattan entertainment community. Full circle moment: years ago, while at Notre Dame, after an aggressive alumni push, I applied to the NY Athletic Club. This 1868 institution has clearly been a beacon of support and structure for amateur sport in our country. In particular, the NYAC is globally renowned for supporting athletes at the highest levels of Olympic Competition, while providing a yesteryear (historic) feel relative to accommodations. However, the main establishment is located at 59th Street and 7th Avenue, dead across from Central Park. Back to my application for membership, almost twenty years ago—there was a mandatory interview. To that end, following a Big East Meeting in Philly, and battling a horrific blizzard, I arrived for my interview as requested in Manhattan. To my surprise, the VP of the nominating committee was a "no show" because of the snowstorm. He couldn't make it into the city from Huntington

(Long Island). Therefore, they conducted the interview by phone. The VP (Huntington guy) apologized like crazy, then went on to tell the group (just a few others) that this interview was merely a "checking the box" exercise, for he said that he knew me since I was a kid, which not only floored me, but left me terribly puzzled. He went on to tell the committee that when we (Huntington and me) were kids, he passed his Newsday paper route on to me. He triggered my memory, and then I remembered him coming to 16 Franklin Street to give me "the book" containing the list of customers, the route, and any other pertinent information. Believe it or not, in exactly the same way, I dropped the Newsday "book of business" off to Ronnie DeFeo (a.k.a., High Hopes) just a few years later.

Of course, each time I visit the NYAC, I get goosebumps from all the Olympic memorabilia. Especially for a USOPC Board Member, it's always quite a rush to visit this athletics cathedral. Finally, to fully close the damn circle, the NYAC enjoys a close relationship with a prestigious golf club called Winged Foot—yes, the same country club where I used to clean carpets as a kid.

We moved around a lot before settling in Amityville, but all of my formative years of schooling took place right there at St. Martin of Tours Catholic Elementary School, Amityville Junior High, and Amityville Memorial High School—class of 1968. Thankfully, it was there that I discovered the power of education.

In sixth and seventh grade, I was blessed to have an amazing teacher, Sister Ann Thomas. She was a Dominican sister from Queens via the mother house in North Amityville. In hindsight, it is clear to me that she had a sixth sense that we suffered from financial instability at home, which is why she tightly monitored my every move. Because of employment transitions, I missed attending kindergarten, and although I was enrolled in the subsequent elementary grades, there was always inconsistency in my attendance. By the time I arrived in the sixth grade, I was way behind and not terribly confident. Sister Ann Thomas put me on an aggressive, hard-nosed program to close the gap. Thus, she taught me the value, if not the emotional impact, of "tough love."

As a schoolboy, I was constantly ill-prepared—my homework was never finished, and unsatisfactory test results often went unsigned by a parent. Consequently, I often found myself incarcerated, for good reason, at the back of the classroom in the coat closet. Sister Ann punished me regularly, for it was clearly warranted. Once, after one too many chastisements for not wearing uniform code black, polished shoes—I decided to wear slip-on "rain rubbers" that were shiny by design and when Sister realized the fact that I had endeavored to beat the system, I was sentenced to the infamous closet for an extended stay. (Years later, when I became totally enamored with the movie, *Cool Hand Luke*, the reference per "spending a night in the box" became symbolic of my St. Martin of Tour's closet existence.) To be sure, "tough love" always modifies behavior, and I am indeed a living example! Quite frankly, this learned reality became a mainstay as a young teacher and coach, and it was indeed a part of my pedagogical tool bag.

Many decades later, circa 2005, while at Notre Dame, I was invited to speak at a mega Catholic fundraiser for the Diocese of Rockville Center in Huntington, Long Island, whereby, in earnest, I referred to Sister Ann Thomas as the educator who saved me from myself and my insecurities. Moreover, since many of the 500 or more attendees were nuns, priests, etc., I asked the audience if anyone knew Sister Ann Thomas, a.k.a., Eileen Donovan. In fact, I conveyed, "If so, please don't ruin the myth, for I remember her being like 6'6 and weighing like 220lbs!"

As I completed my remarks, a former nun rushed up to the podium to let me know that Sister Ann Thomas was her cousin. She also mentioned that Sister Ann left the convent and became a remarkably successful banker at City Bank in Manhattan. Sister Ann Thomas, a.k.a. Eileen Donovan, had a profound, life-lasting impact on many of her former students. I just happened to be one of the select beneficiaries of her "tough love"—she was firmly committed to adolescent growth and development. She had a real gift, and I have referenced her within public conversations for over half a century. To be honest, within my immediate cohort of colleagues, endless staff members, and within our immediate family, Sr. Ann Thomas lived largely. Our family's life has been positively impacted by both the myth and the reality of this exceedingly talented and caring woman.

Another educational turning-point came in the form of Mr. Bush, my junior year guidance counselor at Amityville High School. Coated in naivete, I visited Mr. Bush one day to acquire his insight and advice on where I might attend college. Firmly, with little room for negotiation, Mr. Bush indicated that I could not go to college. He made it clear that, from both a school attendance and academic performance standpoint, college was a non-starter. From there, I began to ponder a military option. I was engaged in a viable conversation with a Marines recruiter, for Vietnam was percolating like crazy, and I held a draft number of 149. My dad had served proudly in the Navy, and his father had been severely injured in WWI as an infantry soldier in the Army. Somehow, this historical calculus computed and began to provide some clarity moving forward. The plan was merely a fleeting thought however, because I was still stuck on going to college. Of course, at that tender age, I thought I could still turn the ship around, for I didn't begin to know what I didn't know. Not to mention the fact that my parents were big-time dreamers, and I was their eldest child. Regardless, Mr. Bush was stern and confident in his analysis.

That wakeup call via Mr. Bush fueled my ambition throughout my entire adult life. Mr. Bush had to be candid with me, and that meeting propelled me almost as much as Sister Ann Thomas empowered me earlier in life. The summer of 1966, I enrolled in five summer school classes at Massapequa High School to make up for the courses I had missed while running Shamrock Dry Cleaners with my father. In addition to earning those lost credits, I somehow passed the NY Regents Exams for those respective courses as well. Once I made up my five-course deficit, I rejoined the secondary school enterprise in the fall and found myself back on track to graduate in the spring of 1968.

Obviously, many decades later, I continue to regale both of these educators –I give full credit to Sr. Ann Thomas and Mr. Bush for my having been in education for fifty-one years, teaching along the way at each and every stop in my career.

> **My good old Amityville days, coupled with the influence of my tremendously passionate and loving parents, somehow presented an ongoing curriculum destined to be reinforced innumerable times on my journey through college athletics.**

Although there were ongoing challenges, my childhood was indeed like a storybook; I was exceedingly fortunate to be nurtured by wonderful folks who totally bought into the American Dream that was ever present in the 50s and 60s. Along the way, I came to subscribe to the theorem that there is strength in numbers. We were a team, and as Ted Lasso would say, "we believed."

The lessons that I learned in the wilds of Long Island largely went unnoticed until I agreed to tackle this book project, which unequivocally took me home.

> **The first, most important truth for a leader to note is that whenever there are multiple human beings involved, competing beliefs and ways of life exist, and they are always in play. Politics exist in every unit, organization, family, team, or community. When any such group cannot press forward as a team—it breaks down and ceases to function. Conversely, when people work together—anything is possible!**

Always aware that my parents and grandparents had no chance of realizing the academic and professional opportunities that I've had, I've been determined to never allow them to slip into darkness; throughout my adult life, I have searched for ways to shine light on their memories and keep them alive in perpetuity. Proudly, I have brought them along as I cut my own life path through entrepreneurialism, entertainment, and sport coupled with my own eager educational pursuit.

CHAPTER 3

DEVELOPING A CAREER: COACHING LESSONS AND REFLECTIONS

"Just do it."

DAN WIEDEN, FOR PHIL KNIGHT/NIKE

Emerson White's sports and entertainment trivia column was a focal point for me as a kid. While my dad was unequivocally a card holding member of sports fandom, I was always more inclined to adorn sport as a participant. From school yard races to church/community picnic competitions, Little League games, and junior high/high school track and field. It was not abnormal to find me practicing alone on my home-made high-jump pit in the backyard, landing on old mattresses. For me, there was always an instinct to compete, whether it be against others or against myself. Some of those competitive occasions occurred in school, like the ongoing annual testing in P.E. class, similar to the President's Council on Physical Fitness; it was important for me to always be the clubhouse leader!

More than participating, competing in sports was always self-gratifying, if not defining for me. Well beyond the individual aspects as described, the social aspect of being part of a team allowed me to enjoy the powerful sense of a mission, whereby the shared objective was about far more than just me. Playing sports as a kid generated an ever-present feeling of both normalcy and connectivity, which I savored.

As for track and cross country, I was always able to run. In terms of events, my running dramatically changed as I physically developed. As a very small junior high kid—like 5'6" and less than 100 lbs.—I could run forever; so, I was slotted into the 880-event training group. Not two years later, when I had physically morphed into 5'8" and 135 lbs., I was moved to the 440. By the time I entered college, I was 5'10.5" and 185 lbs., and I had amassed yet more speed. Therefore, I became a short sprinter in college, while also competing in the 440 whenever needed. My late physical development dictated my competitive reality as I grew older. That said, I always had a love affair with track and became a student of biomechanics and exercise physiology; consequently, it should not have been surprising that by way of family happenstance, I ended up coaching high school and then college track and cross-country. Track was always the place I could easily feel affirmed, if not valued.

Back in the spring of 1968, at the buzzer, a month prior to graduating from Amityville High School, I became intrigued with Jones College in Jacksonville, Florida. A few of my buddies had been admitted and were planning to attend. Given our mutual enthusiasm for surfing and our dedication to the ocean, a last-minute decision to attend a proprietary business school in Jacksonville, Florida, sounded appealing. With nearly no forethought, I applied and was shockingly accepted. (Clearly, they hadn't touched base with Mr. Bush, or anyone else for that matter, at Amityville High.)

Considering my family's financial dynamic, heading to Jacksonville was a real push. Nonetheless, that August, off to Jones College I went along with my surfing buddies. We had been aligned by our physical and spiritual commitment to surfing throughout our adolescence at Gilgo Beach, Hemloch Coves, and occasionally, Montauk. One of the guys, Tony Caramanico, was really gifted. He made a great life out of surfing, winning numerous championships at the Master's level before going on to create a popular line of clothing and high quality surf art.

I attended Jones to close the gap incurred by my lackluster academic background, as well as to continue to elevate myself. In addition to some modest financial aid and a loan, I went back to my childhood roots relative to work, shampooing carpets and waxing floors at night while the rest of the college slept. Fortuitously, I also grabbed a part-time position at Blue Cross Blue Shield as an accounting assistant and occasionally worked as a salesman for the National Shirt Shop at the mall on the weekends.

Upon booking two years of stellar academic performance, combined with a genuine lust to compete on a small college athletics team, I transferred to St. Joseph's College in Rensselaer, Indiana, where I completed my undergraduate degree in business management and marketing while competing on the track team as a sprinter. Amazingly, around ten other Jones students followed me to Rensselaer. It's hard to precisely account for this massive migration, but the other Jones students and I made quite an entrance as we arrived at that small, Catholic college. Naturally, I was provided a stipend and a work-study position shampooing rugs and waxing floors at night—just a creature of habit, I guess. St. Joe's turned out to be the perfect place for me; I continued to close the academic gap and matured emotionally, which occurred by way of meeting my wife, Jane.

One of my favorite courses at St. Joe's was an elective called "Philosophy of Coaching" taught by Professor Bill Jennings (who also doubled as the head football coach). We were assigned to profile two coaching leaders that have captured our imagination, and/or keen interest. For some reason, I found myself researching Frank Kush, ASU Football icon, and Dave Hart Sr., highly touted Athletics Administrator and Coach. Frank was a national news item, and I was interested in Dave because he heralded from a small catholic college, St. Vincent's College, in Latrobe, Pennsylvania.

Decades later, long after Frank was unceremoniously removed from ASU, we formed a relationship, whereby, with higher-up approval, I brought Frank back to ASU from his senior post at the Arizona Boys Home as a special assistant to the Director of Athletics, a position he proudly held almost to the end. As for my other profile subject, Dave Hart Sr.—we have become great friends with the entire Hart family (especially with Dave Hart Jr. and his wife Pam) over the past thirty years. When Dave Jr. was Director of Athletics at East Carolina University, we were busy scheming about what eventually became the creation of Conference USA while I was at Tulane. And years later, we had the pleasure of hosting Dave Sr. at a Notre Dame football game, which was on his bucket list, before he passed. Not sure if Coach/Professor Bill Jennings would say that "the providential hand is clearly at work in our lives," but I will.

May 1972: Jane and Kevin celebrate Kevin's graduation from St. Joseph's College, where he earned a degree in Business Management and Marketing.

Upon graduating from St. Joseph's in 1972, I was hired as a marketing representative for Liggett and Myers Tobacco Company. Ironically, I was onboarded down in Durham, North Carolina. This particular position was secured through a "cold call" interview with an employment agency in Manhattan. As best remembered, being a recent college graduate, I was interested in finding a marketing representative opportunity that would provide a reasonable salary, and perhaps more importantly, a late model automobile—since I lacked the capacity or credit to purchase one in the open market.

Fresh out of school, I took the Long Island Railroad to Gotham City. After a completely off-the-cuff interview, I was offered $7,200K a territory, and a brand-new Dodge Charger. The only complication with the role was that I was vehemently anti-smoking because both of my parents had been life-long smokers and were suffering from different stages of emphysema. As I attended the onboarding sessions in the summer of 1972, my head was spinning. Of course, fast forwarding to 2008—as I arrived at Duke, which was a by-product of the Duke family (legendary tobacco barons), the same private thoughts were indeed reengaged. Although I only maintained that assignment for the summer, I did feel liberated when I transitioned to Monticello, Indiana, in the fall of 1972. My next job was a marketing representative position for a meat packer. To be honest, this location was fueled by Jane's continued matriculation at St. Joe's—for she was a senior, anticipating a 1973 graduation.

December 22, 1972: Jane and Kevin are married in East Tawas, Michigan.

During the preceding summer, Jane and I got engaged and agreed on a December wedding—December 22, 1972—up in East Tawas, Michigan, where her parents lived. With that brewing reality and the fact that Jane had two older brothers whom I greatly admired, we settled in Traverse City,

Michigan. As a former tobacco and meatpacking marketing representative, I found limited professional receptivity in Northern Michigan. However, through Jane's brothers' network, I was fortunate to land two accounting positions at local construction firms—one residential and the other commercial. At that point, Jane was also fulfilling her student-teaching requirement, which allowed her to graduate from St. Joe's in the spring of 1973.

August 1973: Kevin starts his coaching career at Gulf High School in New Port Richey, Florida.

Earlier that year, my parents and siblings relocated from Amityville to New Port Richey, Florida. It was the fastest growing city in the country at the time. My dad, who had long been ill, referred to New Port Richie (NPR) as "God's waiting room!" Upon their relocation, he was diagnosed as terminal. Thus, at fifty-four years old, and without any formal education, my dad was both deathly ill and unemployable. So, the recruiting calls began. My family was upside down in terms of health, finances, and a support system that was familiar, and they wanted to know if we might venture close to New Port Richey to be of help. In a kind of weak moment, Jane and I heeded the distress signal. In short order, we packed up our 1972 VW Bug with all of our possessions to at least discern whether we could create a close-by (to my family) life. This was billed as a "we'll look around and see if a move to that area can be managed"—we never thought we would invest almost four years in NPR.

By August of 1973, Jane and I landed in New Port Richey at my parents' rental house. Pasco County had four or five high schools back in the '70s—today, there are twenty-five. The market was favorably positioned for Jane, a credentialed education major. Jane quickly landed a teaching and coaching

1974: Kevin and Jane White move to Mount Pleasant, Michigan, to coach track and field at Central Michigan University.

job (as in coaching most of the sports sponsored by Clearwater Central Catholic), and I attained a bank trainee position with my business major, all within forty-eight hours of our arrival.

As we regaled our employment success over dinner, Jane unearthed an interesting fact about the local public high school, Gulf High, that caught my attention: she learned that they needed a JV football coach and that, in just two days, they would begin practices in the evenings. With the bank job in hand, I thought about the prospect of coaching after hours.

Jane had aptly described the principal, Dr. Marsh, as a large, balding, middle-aged man with glasses. The next morning, I found myself heading to the teachers' parking lot at Gulf High by 6:30 a.m., on the lookout for Dr. Marsh. As he climbed out of his car, I walked him into his office. Astonishingly, I was offered both a teaching and coaching position by mid-morning. With my dad's failing health, any gainful employment was miraculous.

Dr. Marsh and company secured me a temporary teaching certificate from the state, along with a plan to become permanently certified, which required several additional education credits earned at night.

Not long after I began my teaching and football coaching gig, I was also awarded the head track and cross-country assignment. The only downside was that Gulf High School didn't have a track at the time—we practiced in a driver's education facility on campus. That said, despite the lack of facilities, we had a ridiculous number of kids in the program, and many were naturally gifted athletes. Therefore, realizing unprecedented success was like harvesting low hanging fruit. Our life in Florida was blessed with great students and aspirational families, all of which had recently moved to NPR from all over the country. I loved coaching and quickly discovered that I shared the same passion as Jane for mentoring young athletes. It must be said that Jane was an outstanding high school and college coach. Truly, Jane was very best in class. No joke!

All settled, Jane was a teacher and an extremely popular coach at Clearwater Catholic Central High School (for about $5,500 annually), and I was elated to be hired at Gulf High in NPR, teaching typing and marketing while also coaching football, track, and cross-country. Fortunately, I was already handsomely compensated at $6,750 annually, including the two coaching supplements.

As Jane and I taught and coached by day, we also assumed a portfolio of home-bound students that we taught in the evening at their homes or wherever we could meet. Soon, we purchased a new, small house near my parents for $19,500. Of course, Frankie Marshall, our non-biological uncle, moved down from New York to live with Jane, me, and our first baby, Maureen. A lifelong bachelor via the six-floor Brooklyn walk-up, as well as a hilarious family fixture, "Uncle Frankie" was my dad's best friend. He lived with us on-and-off throughout my life in New York, and then with our young family down in New Port Richey. As they say, the band was back together. Yet, in terms of my dad's condition, the moment was dire.

As I privately think about my forty-seven-year career in sport, thirty-eight years as a director of athletics and nine previous years coaching, I wonder—had I not tackled Dr. Marsh that morning in the parking lot, where might I be today? Before moving down to Florida to help solidify and support my first immediate family, I never really thought about college athletics. Realistically, given my background, I was incapable of even entertaining that prospect.

By the summer of 1974, Jane and I had begun graduate work at Central Michigan University. And while we enjoyed a fair amount of coaching success during the school years at both Clearwater Central Catholic and Gulf, we received a few invitations as a coaching doubles act from various small colleges. We eventually decided to take the plunge and relocate to Michigan in order to coach track at the collegiate level and complete our master's degrees at CMU.

When we left for CMU in 1975, our after-school homebound teaching portfolio was quite expansive. The Superintendent of Pasco County Schools and our good friend, Tommy Weightman, expressed disappointment that we were leaving Florida. Yet, in the same breath, he could not have been more supportive. His immediate concern, however, was about our homebound portfolio. There had never been much interest within the immediate faculty in terms of signing up for that duty. So, as a shot in the dark, I suggested to Tommy that they might consider my father, Emmy White, to both oversee and engage in this ongoing program. I conveyed to Tommy that even though my dad lacked a formal education, he was the brightest individual on the planet. Coupled with his Brooklynite charisma—he would indeed be a rockstar. Tommy got the State of Florida to grant my dad a teaching certificate based on his experience. And so, Emerson James White was provided the distinct opportunity to assume our homebound teaching roles! As I think about my amazing father and how his life circumstances kept him from obtaining a formal education, I find it ironic that, when he died at fifty-eight-years-old in 1976, he was indeed an educator.

Throughout the fifty-eight years that he was "in play," I suspect that his brief teaching tenure represented his proudest professional moment. Not even close! Emmy White's street-intellect instantly made him a rare commodity within the education sector. That short-lived career best defined who he was at the core, while fully celebrating his special gifts.

Allow me to digress here by providing one of the most compelling, if not prideful, moments of my life. Before Jane and I left for CMU, the Gulf High community held a pot-luck dinner in our honor in the school cafeteria. Near the conclusion of the evening, unsolicited, my dad, looking straw thin and well beyond frail, took the floor at his seat, and said something along the lines of, "I am glad to finally be in a position to know how Joe Kennedy must have felt about his children. That's just how I feel about these two!" To be painfully honest, Jane and I feel precisely the same about all five of our kids. It is an overwhelming, if not distinct honor to channel Emmy White, via Joe Kennedy.

To financially support our aspirations in Michigan, Jane took a full-time position at Cadillac High School, teaching and coaching women's basketball. Meanwhile, I volunteered as an assistant track coach at CMU while maintaining a reduced teaching/football coaching load at Cadillac High. Our sixty-mile daily commute was brutal, but the endgame kept us motivated and excited about future opportunities.

Always seeking more responsibility, I was asked to lead the Chip Relays, an annual track meet that attracted several thousand participants annually. For me, the meet will forever stand out in my mind as a singular life-changing moment: I think about it often—how I stood midfield, the circus in full bloom all around me, as a staffer from the office ran over to convey that my dad had passed away. I was paralyzed by the news, sometimes I still am.

Without knowing it, one of the biggest gifts that my dad gave me was the bitterness to remain angry at the world—for Emerson James White was treated so unfairly. Seriously! For my entire adult life, I have been so angry regarding his entire life's story that I never allowed myself to let my guard down. I've always been "at the ready" to debate, to argue, and to fight!

> So, instead, I celebrate all the lessons and inheritances that my tremendous father gave me—primarily, the fortitude to take on all-comers, wherein they will always get my best shot. I loved my father, wish I was half as bright, and would kill to possess his level of unquestionable integrity. He taught me to be relentlessly resilient, and he showed me how to cope and fight.

With all the good NPR/Gulf High connections we had made during our time in Florida, we returned to Gulf High for one more year in order to help settle the family (my mother and three younger siblings) into their new reality following my father's death. The grief was palpable, and anxiety was high; however, new opportunities were ever present. And our favorite "Uncle Frankie" moved back in with us bringing some much-needed comic relief.

As destiny would have it, our family is forever tied to New Port Richey, Florida. Fast forward to 2015: our son, Mike, was offered the Head Basketball Coaching position by Jeremy Foley at the University of Florida. Meanwhile, Jane and I were in Durham, NC, gearing up to host a Board of Trustee dinner at our home. Jeremy Foley was meeting with Mike in Ruston, where Mike was the head coach at Louisiana Tech. Not so mystical, but ridiculously coincidental, a bus pulled up just after we heard the news, whereby all the Duke Trustees disembarked and walked up our driveway. At the front of the Trustee group was Steve and Becky Scott, and Steve happened to be the Chair of the Board at Florida. Of course, we were euphoric about Mike's appointment, but we had been told to keep it a secret; and anyone who knows my wife, Jane, knows that she was totally incapable. Consequently, we felt that we needed to convey to Chairman Scott that Florida just hired a new men's basketball coach before he heard it from the caterer. That evening, following the board dinner, the conversation turned to both Jeremy and Mike (as well as Mike's wife, Kira) wanting us to attend the press conference down in Gainesville that Saturday.

Jane and I were already scheduled to head to the ACC spring meeting down in Jacksonville, Florida, on Friday morning. We were staying at the Ritz Carleton on Amelia Island and determined that we needed to depart at roughly 7:30 a.m. to make the ninety-mile trip to Gainesville in time for the 11:00 a.m. presser. Not unlike past jogs on Amelia Island before daybreak, I preferred to run in the parking garage to avoid critters. To be honest, I have long loved parking garage jogging. Clean. Flat. Well lit. No critters. On this terribly exciting morning, as I began to jog, a face out of nowhere kept appearing and reappearing. It was a portrait out of the past that I could not identify. It looked familiar, but I couldn't connect the familiar dots. After a sixty-minute jog with my newfound friend, I went back up to the room and downloaded to Jane all aspects of this very strange experience. While giving the replay, I asked Jane the name of the head custodian at Gulf High back in the '70's. Jane suggested Jack Mangum, and it instantly clicked. Jane then reminded me that Jack and Silvia (Jack's wife) babysat Maureen (our oldest) and Mike when they were babies while we taught and coached at Gulf HS. With that, we proudly headed to Gainesville to attend the presser. We arrived early and were the first two in the room when a young woman named Megan, who turned out to be a marketing staffer for men's basketball, approached us and asked if we were Mike's parents. Once confirmed, with little hesitation, she said, "I think you knew my late grandparents, Jack and Silvia Mangum." Here we were talking to Jack's granddaughter, Megan Parler, and her husband, Denver Parler, was the men's basketball sports information director. Recounting this wacko occurrence, I still get chills. These crazy, mystical, Celtic visions that come from my grandmother Mariah are truly ever present! And sometimes circumstances bring it to the damn forefront, whereby I am simply forced to acknowledge it.

Back in our final campaign in New Port Richey, I was invited to the University of Tennessee to meet with the great Stan Huntsman, the legendary UT and Olympic track coach. Stan offered me the sprint and hurdle coaching position with the guarantee of an elementary PE teaching position at a nearby public school district. As it happened, while mulling over the UT offer, CMU called to offer the full-time assistant coaching position. Shortly after I accepted CMU's offer, the women's track coach resigned, and they offered the job to Jane.

So, back to the Great State of Michigan we headed. We moved into a farmhouse in Clare, Michigan, with my mother, our first two babies, my brother Terry, Jane's brother David, and my sister Katie. It was a crazy, fun time. On select Sundays, I would have my cross-country team run thirteen miles out to our house from CMU.

When we first arrived at CMU—not unlike the Clampet's with our U-Haul truck jam-packed—we were met at the campus-housing parking lot by the head track coach, Don Sazima. He let us know that he had just accepted the head coaching position for South Korea, and that he would be out-of-pocket for an extended leave. Don was a great coach, a legitimate exercise physiologist, with a significant biomechanics background.

He was a sports scientist. And his assistant, Rollie Ranson, was an absolute wizard! In large part, Don and Rollie had put together an excellent team including Mike Winsor (second place HJ, NCAA, fifth best jump in the world), Bruno Pauletto (National Shot Put Champion), Barry Alexia (world class hurdler), Steve Banovic (800M rockstar), Paul Zucker, Craig Fuller, and so many others.

During my time at CMU, we could take just a large hand-full of athletes and still dominate most meets. With some creativity, we also won most duals, even amongst schools in the Big Ten. The same was true for the women's program; Jane enjoyed tremendous success.

Roy Kramer was the football coach, and Tyrone Willingham coached the defensive backs. Almost immediately, because of my background/experience, I recruited kids that competed in both track and football, wherein Tyrone and I coached some of the same kids during different seasons. In addition, since I was a sprint coach by trade and reputation, I tutored many of the football players in speed enhancement as well.

Over time, I started to recruit kids from Florida—several of my former athletes from Gulf, plus a few exceptionally talented kids from the Tampa Bay area. Herbert Newton was one of the stars from Tampa, among others including my brother, Terry, and sister, Katie. Not to mention, Tom Shaw, America's top speed coach. Poor Tom had to put up with me at Gulf and then again at CMU—his reward should indeed be bountiful!

In 1978, Tennessee's Stan Huntsman was contracted to provide track and field coaching symposiums in Saudi Arabia over the late fall and early winter. There were approximately eight coaching individuals contracted. Late in October of 1978, Stan suffered a serious health setback, and he cold called me to take his place. I felt terribly honored, and also intrigued.

The other coaches and I congressed in London in early November for the orientation. At that time, entrance to Saudi Arabia was limited for Westerners, and the dos and don'ts were graphically depicted. They got my full attention. I will always remember Stan Huntsman fondly for his keen interest in me, and for his unqualified support. As I visit Danny White's office these days at UT, I get goose bumps walking through the track-and-field hall of fame displayed along the walls.

Another tremendous blessing has been my wonderful association over all these years with the United States Sports Academy down in Mobile, Alabama. Dr. Tom Rosandich, and then later his esteemed son, T.J., created a one-of-a-kind, global sports Disney Land of sorts. In addition to contracting countries around the world to facilitate both interesting and complicated projects, they also have a degree granting university at both the graduate and undergraduate level. The Academy's robust curriculum is innovative and global. Years ago, I was honored to provide the commencement address. To be sure, Jane and I were treated like royalty.

By way of the Academy in the late '70s, I was extended an interview to become the head track and field coach for New Zealand. The group of five telephone finalists was narrowed down to three in-person interviews. Unfortunately, Peter Snell and the selection committee identified three other more seasoned candidates than me. However, the Academy didn't give up on me, and around 1979, while they were searching for a new track coach for East Malaysia, I won the contest and realized an offer. But my in-laws, by that time, had lost their sense of humor. Absence of immediate proximity to English speaking grade schools, and all the rest...

In the summer of 1980, with some reluctance, Jane and I accepted the head coaching positions at Morehead State University in Kentucky. Their pitch focused on the fact that Kentucky offered the ideal climate for track and

Summer 1980: Jane and Kevin accept head coaching positions with track and field at Morehead State University in Morehead, Kentucky.

what seemed to be an enhanced programmatic commitment. Only one of those two objectives was realized.

Kentucky is an excellent part of the country for track and cross-country. However, after only being in Morehead for a month, the state dramatically rolled back higher education appropriations. In order to meet this financial reality, MSU dropped track from its roster of sports programming. As you can imagine, Jane and I were totally devastated. Morehead, endeavoring to treat us fairly, offered us full-time faculty positions, which we immediately declined. We chose to put the periscope up and look for a position, or two, back in Michigan. Thankfully, we were invited to the Mount Morris School District. There, I served as the district athletics director, while Jane taught. I oversaw all athletic programs for the district with a lofty pay increase working for legendary superintendent and consummate leader, Dr. Tom Riutta.

Southeast Missouri State (SEMO), in Cape Girardeau, Missouri, then contacted me in the summer of 1981. They were looking for a track coach for their prized program, which had a history of great success and broad community interest. It was hard to not be bitten, once again, by the coaching bug. So, I coached men's and women's track and cross-country while Jane, once again, taught. In addition to coaching, I also oversaw the annual fund, athletics marketing, home contest management, concessions, etc., while also buttoning up my doctorate at Southern Illinois University approximately thirty-miles away. The workload was undeniably heavy, but the precious lessons learned proved to be utterly invaluable.

Like it was yesterday, I remember leading my team in two extended vans across southern Illinois with around fifteen Black student-athletes and one Caucasian student-athlete. It was February 1982, enroute to a big indoor meet in Indiana. We pulled into a small town and attempted to grab breakfast at a local mom-and-pop restaurant. Yet, we were instantly disinvited with the proclamation, "We don't serve those folks in here." Of course, with my NY upbringing, I went ballistic. In defiance, I picked up a chair with designs on throwing it through the front window. As I reflect on my childish behavior, I am embarrassed. The kids grabbed me, and they instantly became the adults in that situation. Sadly, they simply told me that being disinvited was okay, for it wasn't the first time…and it wouldn't be the last.

However, at SEMO, we had tremendous success. We created a huge relay carnival: the *Coors Semotion Relays*. Coors was obviously the major sponsor, and sixty-one colleges and universities participated. The finals were televised and were a gigantic community-wide success. We also had a respectable number of high-profile performers: Rob Thomas (NCAA champion, 600 yards indoor) and innumerable All-Americans (Division I and II). Overall, we nurtured a strong cadre of great track and field athletes, including NCAA Steeple Chase Champion, Mike Vanetta.

As I reflect all these years later, one my proudest achievements was coaching our shuttle hurdle relay team. Pointedly, we had three hurdlers:

Andrew Pressbery, Patrick Mallet, and Leonard Scott (football player). As we got closer to the Relays, the three in hand pushed me to find a fourth hurdler. As we hunted around the team, someone mentioned that one of our managers, Charlie Hinkley, hurdled in high school down in Chaffee, Missouri. As the legend lives on, we entered our new foursome in the Relays and not only won the event, but also qualified for the Drake Relays! At Drake, we found ourselves in the finals among three other blue bloods. We not only won the shuttle hurdle relay event at Drake—one of America's premier track classics—but we also ran the fastest time to date in America (57.4). On the same day, at the Penn Relays, the University of Tennessee bested our time by a smidgen. So, unfortunately, our best time in America was indeed short-lived before Tennessee stole our thunder. Again, when I visit Danny White's office today, all of this vividly comes back to me. Interestingly, the World's Fair was hosted by Knoxville later that summer, and a local bank wanted to match up UT against SEMO in public, on a roadway. Our kids were not terribly enthusiastic. At least one of them subscribed to the "one and done" syndrome, you might guess which one, who I am quite sure wears his Drake Relay watch till this very day.

> **My coaching days helped me understand just how important it is to be empathic, task oriented, adaptable, situational, flexible, and passionate, if not intense. Before being schooled and mentored by Howard Hickey and Dean Stuck, coaching taught me that leadership and politics matter a hell of a lot.**

To be sure, I always loved coaching, and still do. However, once our family began to mature, and as I began to take a deeper dive into academic credentialing, the next logical step seemed to be athletics administration.

Consequently, over the past thirty-eight years, I have served as a director of athletics, although I have never forgotten just how I got here, starting out as a coaching duo with Jane all the way back in New Port Richey.

> **A long way from Toomey's Boat Yard, 16 Franklin Street, and Amityville High, one thing remains clear: teaching, coaching, and athletics administration sure beat working for a living—just ask Patrick O'Donnell, relative to his coal mining exploits.**

Truth be told, those nine years of coaching were my absolute favorite in my elongated career.

When I very privately ponder this circuitous life path, I often think that Sister Ann Thomas would be proud of me, for, in her own way, she was a supreme influencer. Conversely, I wonder whether Mr. Bush, who foreclosed on me as a teenager for good reason, had any idea that he actually helped light the damn fuse.

Howard Hickey, a leadership theorist at Michigan State, and Dean Stuck, a political theorist at Southern Illinois University, had an incalculable impact on me during my graduate studies. Hickey and Stuck taught me theory, if not a few practical techniques relative to both politics and leadership based on empirical data, which clearly impacted my professional career. Dr. Howard Hickey formally provided me with the empirical affirmation to support my practices to date. And Hickey developed in me the mindset that leadership is inherent, but that it can also be cultivated.

> **More specifically, Leadership is art form; conversely, management is a science.**

Managers can be taught specific behaviors and skills, whereas leaders are born. In recent years, I have espoused that the two things a leader cannot delegate are being the discernible leader (unquestionably) and managing all of the competing political forces (you will see this come up in later chapters). Practically, I believe that I nurtured those competencies, before ever learning the theory, through coaching.

As for my doctoral dissertation topic, Title IX, Jane and I learned first-hand about the inequity in sport beginning with Jane's compensation compared to mine, wherein she was appreciably more successful as a high school and college coach. Actually, for Jane, sport inequity first impacted her as a young athlete when she was not given a real opportunity to compete. At St. Michael's, where she attended high school in Flint, Michigan—Jane successfully brought a group of girls together and approached the athletic director to ask if they could form an intramural basketball team and she even got him to arrange for them to play against the other catholic high schools in the area. She continued to play intramural basketball at St. Joseph's College, but there was no opportunity to compete against other colleges in her day. This is all to show how badly Title IX was needed, and just how late it arrived for many women.

> **Of all the advanced curriculums that I have been duly touched by, education is the prized element of my crazy life and career path.**

Therefore, I am a hard-charging proponent of maintaining the educational component within the student-athlete experience. It can't just be all about entertainment, for that will represent an unfulfilled life for the participants. More on this critical subject as we fartlek forward.

CHAPTER 4

LORAS COLLEGE: BECOMING THE LEADER

"Fear will be the fuel for all your success, and the root cause of all your failures, and the underlying dilemma in every story you tell yourself about yourself. And the only chance you'll have against fear? Follow it. Steer by it. Don't think of fear as the villain. Think of fear as your guide, your pathfinder—your Natty"

J.R. MOEHRINGER, THE TENDER BAR

With a cupboard full of purple and gold cups, my thirty-eight-year director of athletics career began in June of 1982 at Loras College in Dubuque, Iowa, home of the Rock Bowl, bratwursts, and light beer on ice.

A few months prior to our move in the spring of '82, I was a graduate student finishing up my doctorate at Southern Illinois while coaching track and field at Southeast Missouri State. Before graduation, I was contacted by a few small colleges about vacant athletic director positions. Most notably, Loras College grabbed my attention because it was a diocesan college, and my great, longtime friend, Joe Piane (who was a seasoned track coach at Notre Dame) was a distinguished Loras graduate. Further, many years earlier, Loras had recruited Jane and me to coach track and cross-country. In any event, I was not yet ready to separate from coaching collegiate track—the idea of leaving coaching just wasn't emotionally doable. So, although we fell in love with their institutional mission, I turned down the Loras offer.

Then, roughly a month after my dismissal of their offer, Dr. Pat DiPasquale, president of Loras, circled back and courted me once again. The more Jane and I talked about it, the more the job made sense. At the time, our family was growing, and it was becoming clear that athletics administration was our professional endgame. So, off to Loras College we went.

June 1982: Kevin White, at age 31, proudly takes on his first administrative role as Athletic Director at Loras College in June 1982, a milestone he fondly remembers as "You always remember your first."

Upon arriving in Dubuque, it was clear to me that the institution was floundering. Loras Athletics was all but non-descriptive within the community, on top of being seriously under-resourced. Having already accepted the responsibility to build and enhance athletics, I only then really understood the challenge I had undertaken. Loras College was also suffering from stagnant enrollment in those days, so re-legitimatizing the institution via athletics became a compulsion. Therefore, as a snot-nosed thirty-one year-old athletic director and a recovering track coach, I found myself clamoring for a "point of difference" to launch the next era of Duhawk Athletics.

In an attempt to better learn the lay of the land, I desperately sought out the institutional powers that impacted life at the college. I needed to have a clear understanding of what I was walking into: what resources (financial and otherwise) were available to me, and what benchmarks were expected to be met. Moreover, because of Dean Stuck's political curriculum, I was desperate to locate the origin of the power, if not utter institutional influence, whereby all futuristic decisions emanated that would impact the life of the college.

Political theorists espouse that there are two basic types of power: formal and informal. Formal power is exercised by an ascribed authority figure, for they have been duly codified as the leader. This is an overt form of power. Informal power, however, is exercised by informal systems, which can be rather covert and/or discreet. That said, shortly after my arrival, I made the rounds speaking to the formal players: president, chancellor, board chair, faculty senate chair, looking for an infusion of resources to expedite the moving forward plan as envisioned. Through a series of conversations, it became evident to me that an enhanced athletics program could serve as an extension of admissions, while also raising the level of institutional awareness in general.

In the fall of 1982, I diligently began attending all faculty and staff summits. And the trend was painfully clear: at each meeting, some segment of the college would provide their next visionary iteration, which always had an accompanying price tag. Listening to my colleagues, I felt their desperation. After all, resources within the athletic department were badly incommensurate with programmatic, departmental, *and* institutional expectations. In college athletics, if not across all organizations, if you are undercapitalized, you will never realize optimal success—an organization may catch lighting in a bottle, but it won't be sustainable.

After about three all-staff meetings, it became clear to me that Bud Noonan, the Loras registrar, was the unspoken peacekeeper of the bunch. When squabbles over limited funds naturally ensued, Bud would calm the room. He'd typically restate the case and, at times, offer a potential solution. Without fail, Bud's common-sense reaction and approach would always carry the room.

Bud was a lifer at Loras; he wasn't a terribly pedigreed academic, but he was clearly the smartest individual in the room. He was humble to a fault and a beloved servant leader. It would have been difficult, perhaps implausible, to identify Bud Noonan as the most powerful influencer in the greater Loras College community. However, unbeknownst to Bud, he wielded enormous informal power.

Taking note of such, I began taking Bud out to lunch. Over our meals, I spoke about a sizable infusion of college resources into athletics. It was evident to me that an enhanced athletics program at Loras could serve as an extension of admissions, while also raising the level of general institutional awareness within the wider Dubuque community. I promised a considerable ROI based on admissions, connectivity to the community, alumni engagement, and the support of local businesses. Needless to say, Bud was intrigued.

In January, at one of the first all-staff meetings of the year, I was invited to make my futuristic case for Loras Athletics. Predictably, as I spoke candidly about an enhanced financial investment in the department, the fur flew! As I stood in front of the group, vulnerable to attack, I believed General Custer to have had better odds.

Then, as if it were choreographed, Bud Noonan stood up at the end of my presentation and said that he had listened to my vision and thought it had merit. Instantly, the mood of the room changed *radically*.

> **At the end of the day, throughout that first fall and winter, it had become terribly obvious to me that two things were painfully true: 1) college athletics is highly politicized and 2) to endure, and more importantly to flourish, an effective leader must have a fairly high political IQ.**

If there is a third belief here, it is that an apolitical leader won't last very long. It's hard to say whether my political instincts were inspired as a kid working through an under-resourced upbringing or as a young coach. No matter their origin, they proved to be a primary component of my everyday life as an athletic administrator.

Having successfully weathered the frenzy of the Loras College all-staff meeting, I walked away with my head held high and the promise of funding à la Bud Noonan's endorsement. While feasibly meager, it was funding, nonetheless.

We were off to the races!

In addition to Bud Noonan, another unlikely ally soon emerged on campus; the academic icon and renowned critic of college athletics who arguably became my best friend and closest confidant during my tenure was none other than Fr. Karl Schroeder. Fr. Schroeder was a noted Shakespeare Scholar and the Cecil DeMille of Loras College, wherein he created a highly regarded dance/entertainment troop that toured the country. He could be tough; legend has it that his students were terrified of him. But he could also be shockingly brilliant and hysterically funny in the same breath. In addition, Father Karl was a film advisor/consultant for both *Going My Way* and *Bells of St. Mary's*, not to mention a great friend of Walt Disney. With my mother's entertainment background, I somehow got a hall pass (from the anti-athletic Father Karl wrath). Fr. Karl frankly loathed athletics, but he was somehow smitten by our family. No doubt his endorsement of me softened a few key faculty members and administrators. He'd often invite us to his Rohlman Hall apartment for his famous ten-minute liturgy and social afterwards, which consisted of Blatz beer, scotch, and ruffles in a Tupperware bowl. He was such a blessing to me, and I'll never know how or why I was able to win him over—as far as I know, Jane and I were the only friends he ever had who were tied to athletics. However, no college or university has ever had a better, more seriously connected, or highly influential asset than Father Karl.

> **Since my early coaching days, and to an even greater degree when I transitioned to my long administrative tenure, leading/managing what I might refer to as the "human condition" has been, unequivocally, a top priority.**

When in doubt, I leaned into my father's examples of winning people over.

When we began laying out our department's goals, my team and I observed a few blatant facts. Paramount among them, we saw a clear gap between the college and the community. This gap, we believed, could be bridged via athletics.

Dubuque is one of the most Catholic towns in which I've ever lived. (It rivals, and maybe even beats out, South Bend!) In the '80s, there were lots of big families, kids outside playing and running through the neighborhoods until dark, and a parish with an attached parochial school for nearly every square mile. The community was already connected, so if a college (especially a Catholic college) caught their attention, the fever would potentially spread quickly.

Competing for visibility is an active ongoing pursuit for college athletics. Branding—or perhaps better said, enhanced branding—is a sport unto itself; it literally affects all dimensions of the athletics enterprise. The task that lay at our feet was a sizable one, but I knew this challenge all too well.

One way to generate a sizable branding or rebranding effect is to create a major event, which may stir the pot, and create excitement before high profile competitive success occurs. Highlighting the talent of Loras's student athletes and capitalizing on the excitement of competition would force a natural marriage between the community and its Catholic college. In fact, I'd seen the results of such events before.

Back in 1974, as the track coach at Gulf High School in New Port Richey, I'd created the Chasco Fiesta Relays. The school had just been given the money to build a brand-new track, and we wanted to excite the community. So, we formed a major track meet and heralded the fact that we had a really great group of high-quality sprinters. This one-day event produced a very large crowd, and the track program instantly garnered great local interest and support.

Then, back in 1982, at Southeast Missouri State, we created the Coors Semotion Relays, where sixty-one track and field teams ascended on Cape Girardeau, Missouri, for an event sponsored by Adolf Coors. With Charlie Besser's help, the finals were televised. The event proved to be great for the city, the university, and SEMO track and field.

The huge success of these past events gave me confidence that something similar would work in Dubuque. Hence, the National Catholic Basketball Tournament (NCBT) for small catholic colleges was reborn in 1983.

The original NCBT had been last held in 1952. Over thirty years later, sixteen men's teams and sixteen women's teams all traveled to Dubuque, Iowa, in early January for the event. Anheuser Busch was the sponsor and Charlie Besser, my dear friend, managed to put the NCBT finals on television, whereby luminaries like Al McGuire, Joe B. Hall, "Easy Ed" Macauley, Dick Vitale, Billy Packer, Hank Raymonds, Cardinal Bernardin, and many others made our crazy catholic fest come to life. The town of Dubuque and the state of

Iowa quickly embraced the event. The NCBT was deemed "the special event of the year" for three years running by Terry Branstad, then Governor of Iowa.

All this to say, the NCBT was a huge success! We were able to effectively jumpstart momentum through alternate means while engaging the community like never before. Due to the tremendous support of my colleagues—Loras College Alumni President Chip Murray, Associate Athletic Director Jan Leiser, and Administrative Assistant Jane Specht—the NCBT accomplished one of our primary departmental and programmatic goals despite our severe lack of resources.

Regarding Networking: many years post Loras, I arrived at Arizona State and served as an interim chair of the Pac 10 Men's Basketball Committee, where four former NCBT coaches were proudly sitting around the table: Ben Braun (California) via Siena Heights University, Eddie Payne (Oregon State), and later Kevin Eastman (Washington State) via Belmont Abbey College, and Kevin O'Neill (USC) via Marycrest College. All of which, as recovering NCBT coaches, had an indelible impact on college basketball.

Outside of athletic administration, I first began to understand the basics of human resources and talent acquisition while at Loras College. Given the school's predominately white demographic, there was an utter absence of Black and Brown folks represented in leadership on campus. Recognizing this lack, we hired Charlie Taylor, a former Southeast Missouri State long jumper, who served as Director of Minority Affairs; he also served as an assistant coach for track and football. *I believe he was the first person of color ever hired at Loras College.*

Historically, Loras College, founded in 1839, enjoys a long-standing history with the University of Notre Dame. Pointedly, the relationship between Father Edwin Sorin (ND) and Bishop Mathias Loras (Loras) originated in

France, and continued through ongoing communication between Indiana and Iowa. They shared higher education strategies, as well as key staffers as the institutions were indeed fermenting. And as a highly coveted piece of, under-utilized, relationship history—both institutions had a supreme impact on the emergence of catholicity in the upper Midwest, specifically on the evolution of the Archdiocese of both Chicago and Minneapolis.

As for Loras Athletics, there was a serious trend to recruit head coaches from the practice football fields in South Bend. Shortly after arriving at Loras, I met with a long-retired cleric, Monsignor Michael Martin, who had been President of Loras after serving in a variety of institutional roles, including serving as a highly celebrated pastor in Dubuque. Back in his undergraduate days at Loras, Monsignor Martin (as a student) served on the first football head coaching selection committee. As the story goes, Monsignor, along with a few priests, took the Zepher over to the practice fields at Notre Dame to go "coach shopping." On one such mission, they were instantly enamored with Notre Dame's rockstar assistant football coach and chemistry teacher, Knute Rockne. Unfortunately for the Loras search committee, the feeling was not mutual, so the committee transitioned to option "B": Charles Emile "Gus" Dorais who served as head football coach at Loras (then Dubuque College) from 1914 to 1917.

However, in 1915, Dorais played professional football alongside Rockne for the Massillon Tigers and after a late November Tigers game in Toledo, Rockne joined Dorais for the long train ride back to Iowa and offered to help coach Loras (Dubuque College at the time) in the Thanksgiving Day rivalry game against crosstown foes, Dubuque German. While the outcome of the game was not favorable for Loras, Rockne did in fact coach the Duhawks for one game—providing yet another connection between the "Purple and Gold" and the "Fighting Irish."

Then, later, Loras returned to the ND practice fields to recruit Eddie Anderson, who served as head football coach from 1922 to 1924, before once again traveling back to ND to recruit Elmer Laydon (1925/1926), then jumping on the Zepher to land Jerry Jones (1932/33), and back again to snag John Niemiec (1934 to 1937). Finally, the last ND assistant to serve as the Loras head coach was Wally Fromhart (from 1947 to 1950). Throughout that era, Loras College was fondly referred to as "Little Notre Dame." In turn, Loras insiders have often quipped over the years that they fondly refer to Notre Dame as "Big Loras"!

Ironically, while I served at Loras, a number of Loras individuals would, within overly (embarrassingly) generous attributions, suggest that I would become the Notre Dame Athletic Director one day. To be painfully honest, as a non-alum, that silly chatter was considered to be a nonstarter, until Gene Corrigan's shocking overture (on behalf of Father Monk Malloy) years later while we were at ASU. I wondered then if that surreal invitation was indeed being orchestrated by our long line of Irish ancestors, including my parents and grandparents; or, if Jim Crowley had a hand in this unthinkable circumstance from above—recounting our truly savored luncheon at the infamous Ho Jo's in upstate New York.

Given Loras College and Dubuque, Iowa's rich history relative to the Catholic Church, as historically appointed, the archbishop of the diocese serves as the chancellor of the institution. Coincidentally, in 1983, Daniel Kucera, OSB, became archbishop of Dubuque and chancellor of Loras College. A recovering college president, the archbishop became not only supremely interested in the mission of Loras College, but also in the progression of me and my career. Within a year of his appointment, Archbishop Dan began speaking with me about becoming a college president. During one of our conversations, he referenced the Institute for Educational Management (IEM) at Harvard, a post-graduate program designed for individuals that aspired to leadership roles within higher education.

Before I knew it, Archbishop Dan had pushed me to apply. My attendance in Cambridge, Massachusetts, was surely an eye-opener for someone who not long before had lived a life with stop watches and batons. Within the ninety-two matriculants in 1985, I was the only individual with an intercollegiate athletics background; therefore, I became the resident athletics expert. It was truly a brilliant experience for a young, aspirational leader.

Not long after I returned from Harvard, I was summoned to Archbishop Dan's office. Given his motivation, along with President Pat DiPasquale, I was *told*—"Father knows best"—that I would become the dean of students/vice president of student affairs. Understandably, I was devastated to leave behind the athletics department. So, as a bit of a concession, I was told that I could remain closely aligned with Loras Athletics via the NCBT.

Not a year later, Archbishop Dan summoned me to his office to let me know that I would become the vice president for institutional advancement, with the same athletics concession as before. Even after all these years, I remember vividly pushing back, for these promotions felt like a real divorce from coaching. As I respectfully protested, Archbishop Dan clearly and authoritatively responded, "I am not asking you, I am telling you!" Consequently, my brief tenure in student affairs was terminated, and I went forth into advancement.

As I continued to build the development team, I was most fortunate to recruit Jim Collins as a development officer. Years later, I was terribly honored to serve on the Loras Board, while Jim Collins served as the college's esteemed president, which he has been for the past twenty-five years. Jim Collins is a rockstar who truly defines servant leadership!

I fully recognized back then, and perhaps to an even greater degree today, that Loras represented a bit of a laboratory for me to practice the lessons of my ancestral heritage coupled with the leadership and political theory I harvested at both Michigan State and Southern Illinois. This leadership opportunity wherein resources were clearly incommensurate with expectations was the *perfect* first appointment.

Reflecting on my first role as an athletic director, I recognize that it was actually the first time I was called upon to be a consummate leader beyond coaching. Given my lack of readiness to lead, let alone manage, the affairs of a small college athletics department at thirty-one years old, I can only say that I was very well supported by the existing staff, both coaching and administrative. For a leader with overt aspirations, transitioning from NAIA to NCAA Division III, this became a classic "loaves and fishes" operation; the core administrative team, which was truly spectacular, had to engage in all the respective activities and responsibilities, with the leader closely connected and aligned. Thus, my professional growth could not have been better served. There were so many great individuals at Loras, and President DiPasquale could not have been a better mentor.

Pointedly, when I became athletic director in 1982, Loras only had eleven sports. Throughout the interview process, there was at least some recognition that an expanded athletics portfolio would favorably impact enrollment, for, in 1982, the enrollment was only 1,300 from a once upon a time high water mark of around 1,800. When I left Loras in 1987, five years later, the enrollment jumped to just under 2,000—the move from eleven sports to *twenty* was most impactful!

Given that, the two things I gleaned the most from my Loras College leadership experience was that I could not delegate the responsibility per being the leader, and I, personally, had to manage the competing political forces (at the risk of being repetitive, this key lesson comes up a lot). No one else could do either one of these critical endeavors for me.

> **Finally, if there was a third thing that became clear to me, it was the importance of gaining the power and influence of a seasoned network.**

Early in my administrative journey, I quickly unearthed NACDA (National Association of Collegiate Directors of Athletics), where I obtained an informal graduate degree relative to being an athletic director. Both the formal and informal education harvested, in addition to the network, and/or brotherhood/sisterhood, was indeed priceless for an administrative neophyte. Via NACDA, I enjoyed the opportunity to rub shoulders and interact with the giants of the industry, which over my almost four-decade career as a director of athletics would prove to be simply invaluable.

Finally, we proudly began to train a few future athletic directors (AD) back in Dubuque: Thomas Boeh (Ohio University and Fresno State), Tim Van Alstine (Western Illinois and Cardinal Stritch), Bob Bierie (twenty-five year Head Football Coach, and then AD—truly a Loras College legend), and Greg Capel (Loras). These four individuals are the founders of a long list of AD superstars we quite regularly churned out along this wild journey.

I will forever love Loras College. After all, you always remember your first. Undoubtedly, I am most grateful for all of the leadership and political experiences rendered in those years as a green AD. And perhaps most impactfully, we learned to *Do a Little Duhawkin!* And for that, I will be eternally grateful.

CHAPTER 5

UNIVERSITY OF MAINE: ARTICULATING THE VISION

"Management is doing things right;
leadership is doing the right thing."

PETER DRUCKER

After completing the IEM (Institute for Educational Management) program at Harvard, where I was the lone participant with direct athletics experience, I garnered an unanticipated network, which led to being invited as a preferred candidate for two Division I director of athletics positions. First, I was targeted for an interview at Fordham University as one of four finalists thanks to the long-standing vice president at Fordham, my IEM classmate Jay McGowan. However, the position was rightly awarded to Frank McLaughlin, the then head men's basketball coach at Harvard. Frank, as a celebrated Fordham alum, was the perfect choice. Several months later, another IEM classmate, Tom Aceto, vice president at University of Maine, invited me to participate in the AD search at Maine. Interestingly, both Jay and Tom eventually became extraordinarily successful, long-term college presidents.

As I took part in the interview process at Maine, I could detect that there was some leaning toward securing an alum, of which there were several in the final pool. Upon realizing the opportunity to interview in the initial round, the search committee passed along only three of the four finalist names to President Dale Lick. Unfortunately, at that moment, I didn't make the cut. Most surprising to me, I received a private phone call from President Lick asking me to meet him in Portland, Maine, for lunch. We spoke for a few hours, and just prior to the end of our lunch, Dale offered me the job. This did not sit well with the local establishment, alumni, or media, to say the very least.

Of course, it wasn't easy leaving Loras for many reasons. We had no history in Maine, but we fell in love with the pristine environment and peerless landscape. And it wasn't difficult to become excited about the programmatic potential across all sports, especially with the unqualified support of President Lick and Vice President Aceto.

> **At Maine, once again, we took immense pride in doing more with less—a "loaves and fishes" assignment, if you will. This method of making the most out of the least has been a talent that I've fortuitously honed over my time as an AD, and it was surely well tested and practiced in Maine.**

We inherited a terrific administrative staff and added some key players to this overachieving team in our first few months at Maine. The charge, and/or objective, was daunting, but finding a way to move the needle dramatically within an under-resourced framework had long become our way of life.

It was at Maine that I first really understood the power—if not the value—of HR as a functionality. We not only tried like crazy to recruit the best, most seasoned individuals, but to also, through a series of reorganizations and staff development, diligently place each player in just the right position to ensure their discernible success.

I suspect that, across most collegiate franchises back then—which I believe would also be true today—about twenty-eight percent of an athletic department's budget was tied to compensation for staff and coaches. Keeping that fact in mind, as an athletic director, I was faced with two different options: 1) use our money wisely by ensuring that all employees were working in a singular direction or 2) allow the fractional forces to stop our department from realizing optimal success. Employing a culture built on two-way communication, candor, and truth-telling while also providing ample opportunity to support the articulated vision is paramount.

1987: Kevin White is named Athletic Director at the University of Maine, Orono, where he served from 1987 to 1991.

The second most significant lesson I learned while at Maine was the inherent need to monitor compliance. When I arrived at Maine, Black Bear Ice Hockey was competitively outstanding, with a trajectory to become even more successful. The coach, Shawn Walsh, was a dynamo—as good as it gets. Shawn was bright, charismatic, and inordinately passionate about the plight of Maine Ice Hockey. Clearly, one of the best in the business, and he was adored by his players, all of whom came to Maine because of Shawn.

However, during the fall of 1987, just a few months after my arrival, it was clear to me that our *Friends Ice Hockey Group* was providing players with extra benefits. Of course, today that permissive activity is without guardrails and/or any clear and concise NCAA regulations, so it would indeed be permissible, if not fully expected. Given that this was not okay at the time, I invited a few NCAA staff members to our campus in Orono to assess our purported behavior and provide the department and/or university with the proper guidelines needed to move forward. As we rewired our compliance program, it caused some anticipated/predictable friction between Shawn and me. Despite the conflict, I know that I would do precisely the same thing today should I find myself in a similar position.

> **As the leader, I accepted the responsibility to protect the image and reputation of the institution.**

It takes many decades to build an image and/or reputation, and it only takes a nanosecond to burn that reputation to the ground. Maine, a proud "Public Ivy," could not have accepted the aforementioned hit to their brand.

Many years after I left, the NCAA nailed Maine for non-compliant activity, along with suspending Shawn for a year. Shawn reached out to me and asked if I might intervene for him with the NCAA infractions committee, which I did. Shawn was indeed a supreme talent, and I loved working with him. Not terribly long after he was reinstated, he contacted me from UCLA (University of California, Los Angeles) Medical in Los Angeles; he was staying at Goldie Hawn and Kurt Russell's home, dealing with the prospect of a terminal illness. He asked me to fly out and spend a day with him, which I was honored to do. While there, Shawn said he had always wanted to attend a Notre Dame football game and asked if he could bring his two sons and sit with me in my box. Of course, they came, stayed at our house, and sat with me for the first half; however, Shawn did not have another half in him, for he became extremely sick, I suspect from the chemo. That was the last time I saw Shawn Walsh. We were great Celtically aligned colleagues on my very first day up in Orono, and again during our final visit at Notre Dame stadium.

Another crucial HR compulsion for me has been DEI/pluralism. Earlier, I spoke about my organic inclinations, if not, nonnegotiable commitment around this complicated space. With that said, I can very honestly say that over the past thirty-eight years as a college director of athletics, there isn't anything that has given me more satisfaction than advancing and supporting underrepresented populations! This activity stems from employing an earnest pre-procurement level of effort. Suffice it to say, I was always window-shopping, keeping an eye on the market.

Within athletics, sometimes the search process needs to be expedited for recruiting reasons, and today, for transfer portal reasons. Managing a roster necessitates having a high-quality leader "in play"! This clearly applies to both coaching and administrative talent. Once you identify the process, as well as the characteristics the position warrants, the procurement function becomes paramount. At Maine, with minimal resources, we worked with HR diligently and tried to get a serious return on investment. Finally, the least formally practiced piece of HR is integration. It is critically important to create a vibrant, thoughtful, if not creative, onboarding strategy to place your new/next leader in a position to be most successful. When a department or institution experiences a short-term tenure, in almost every case, the integration part of the process was underworked and/or the leader did not manage all the competing political forces very well, or perhaps both. Within college athletics, roughly a third of the annual expense budget is driven by coaches and staff compensation. Therefore, this piece of the administrative puzzle warrants a leader's supreme attention.

At Maine, with minimal resources, we worked diligently with HR to hire the very best in the biz. Upon my arrival on campus in 1987, I quickly made two basketball head coaching changes. One was related to a long tenure, and the other was based on allegations of serious misconduct. These two searches were not far removed from one another. We hired Rudy Keeling from Marquette as the men's basketball coach, and Trish Roberts from Tennessee as the women's basketball coach; both were assistants at solid programs, and both happened to be African American. From this moment on, I was characterized as a NY liberal and the wacko editorials with cut-out letters began arriving in the mailbox, warning us about the respective safety of our kids when they walked to school. Predictably, as the saga materialized at Maine, they were the first two head coaches of color at any college or university in Maine, where the ethnic minority population was around a fourth of a percent at that time.

The late Rudy Keeling became director of athletics at Emerson College before becoming commissioner of the ECAC (Eastern Collegiate Athletics Conference). Trish Roberts, a former Olympian and All-American, took over from a long-standing male coach. In my career as an AD, I proudly—by design—never hired a male to coach a female sport.

> **In my humble view, if college athletics is in the leadership development business, then the representation of heavily qualified individuals representing the large, eclectic universe of student-athletes is indeed essential.**

This process is percolating, but vigilance must be maintained.

We enjoyed pretty darn good hiring success at Maine, and a good number of our staffers became ADs: Thomas Boeh, who came with me from Loras (Ohio University and Fresno State University); Jim Sterk (Portland State University, Washington State University, San Diego State University, University of Missouri, and Western Washington University); Tim Van Alstine (Western Illinois University and Cardinal Stretch University); Ian McCaw (Northeastern University, University of Massachusetts, Baylor University, and Liberty University); Mark Wilson, an intern on our staff (Tennessee Tech); Anne McCoy (Washington State); and Janet Lucas (California Northridge and Pacific University).

On the coaching side of the ledger, our record was equally impressive: Rudy Keeling, Trish Roberts, Tim Murphy (esteemed head football coach at Harvard for thirty years, also at Cincinnati and Maine), Kirk Ferentz (the longest continuous FBS coach, and the highly celebrated head football coach at Iowa for over thirty years), the late Tom Lichtenberg (Morehead State University and Ohio University); and Buddy Teevens (Dartmouth, Tulane, Stanford, and Maine).

To be fair, at both Southeast Missouri and at Loras, fundraising became a significant part of my professional existence. However, at Maine, resource acquisition became a mainstay of my administrative life. For me, fundraising is but a subset of resource acquisition. A leader and/or the leadership team must constantly chase all the pieces of potential revenue—traditional, non-traditional, and philanthropic—with the goal of making sure that the pool of resources is indeed commensurate with the programmatic expectations and/or the experience marketed to the prospective student-athlete. If an athletics administrator accepts the premise that resources (including facilities) must be at least somewhat commensurate with programmatic expectation in order to support the institutional mission as well as meet the marketed expectations of today's savvy student-athletes, then acquisition and finance warrants a very high priority relative to day-to-day functioning.

Maine was fairly impoverished back in 1987. While it was a proud and pristine environment, the state was painfully poor. To be blunt, with a smaller population and a limited number of wealthy individuals who live in the state, closing the historic gap between the financial reality and programmatic expectations was indeed a massive undertaking. Upon my arrival as an individual "from away"—as I was antagonistically coined—I quickly realized that Maine would require a heavy lift in terms of resource acquisition and fundraising. My esteemed Professor Dean Stuck's mentoring came in handy, for as we endeavored to create a forwardly vision, we also began to look for prospective investors to bring that vision to life.

Our first investor was Harold Alfond, the founder and CEO of Dexter Shoe and a limited partner of the Boston Red Sox. After we secured Harold's support, we unearthed Larry Mahaney, the CEO of Webber Oil and a staunch UM alum. Incidentally, Harold and Larry were joined at the hip relative to supporting the great state of Maine, as well as the educational aspirations of prospective in-state students. As I reflect on those days, I learned a great deal, both politically and philanthropically from Maine's version of Bob Wallace and Phil Davis (*White Christmas*).

As a young AD, my interactions with Harold were intense: he typically wanted to provide partial funding for significant projects with an unequivocal guarantee that "things" would eventually all work out in the end. Harold always came through on his promise, returning to our projects and donating all but the full allotment of needed resources. Almost immediately upon meeting, Harold took a keen interest in me, if not in my chutzpah. Jane and our kids became regular attendees at Alfond family functions shortly thereafter, and conversations surrounding the financial facilitation of an aspirational athletics vision occurred frequently and freely.

The late Harold Alfond is the state of Maine's most generous philanthropist and a mega benefactor to the University of Maine, specifically to Black Bear Athletics. Several years ago, the Harold Alfond Foundation provided UMaine with a $320M gift—$170M of which was directed to athletics. This was quite possibly the largest single philanthropic gift to a public university ever! Harold loved Maine, its people, his esteemed family, and college athletics in general. The Harold Alfond Foundation has been incredible, providing a $500 grant to every newborn in Maine for higher education, just to mention one significant Foundation commitment that will live in perpetuity. To be frank, I could write a book on Harold, and pointedly show the effect he had on our entire family. To say that we loved Harold—a brilliant mentor, close friend, and a terribly generous benefactor—is truly an understatement. He became a bit of a surrogate father to me.

Over the years, even after I left Maine, Harold provided unsolicited resources to Tulane, Arizona State, and Notre Dame. Harold was pretty bashful, so I would also be called upon, regardless of my location, to deliver "ribbon cutting" remarks wherever Harold had donated a gymnasium, baseball complex, hospital cancer center, and an endless number of other major benefactions. We savor our experience with this great American family, and Harold and Bibby Alfond continue to lend support from "on high" at an extraordinarily high level! The crux of this missive is intended to portray the power of relationship, if not, connectivity: don't ever underestimate the value of relationships!

Larry Mahaney was a force of nature in his own right. Between Harold and Larry, the entire athletics campus was re-invigorated. Harold and Larry (Wallace & Davis) influenced so many capital projects, it would take a stand-alone book to detail the complete inventory.

A sizable breakthrough moment occurred when we were contemplating repurposing the Harold Alfond Arena, including the construction of a small number of suites. As usual, Harold committed to providing the lion share of funding needed for the project. However, it required the pre-selling of the suites to close the financial gap, and it became clear that there were few in-place benefactors with the ability to jump into our collective vision.

Then, Larry directed me to Stephen King, who, at that point, was not closely affiliated with his alma mater, or Black Bear Athletics for that matter. Getting in to see Stephen proved to be a challenge, but he eventually agreed to meet with me in his office near the airport. It was a humble steel building, and I waited in an outer-office while he finished a conference call in his private office. With permission, I facilitated his eight-track while I waited and played some Bob Dylan. When he finally walked out, I could see that he was not eager to hear my sales pitch. In fact, he very candidly suggested that he was not particularly interested in pre-purchasing a suite.

However, after a reasonably long exchange, Stephen walked me to my car and we bonded slightly over our mutual fondness for Bob Dylan. Suddenly more receptive, he asked, "How much are the suites again?" I told him, "$125,000 for ten years, payable over three or five years." Stephen then pulled out his checkbook and paid the full amount upfront. Thanks to Uncle Bob, he instantly committed.

Once Stephen committed, the rest of the suites sold instantaneously, which enormously affected the philanthropy warranted to either build or makeover a good number of athletics projects. In Dean Stuck's political theory, he states that the number ones influence the number twos, who in turn influence the threes, who then shape and influence the fours, and so on. The lesson here is that a leader must identify who shapes and influences an institution, department, or organization. The leader, or leadership team, must be able to make the case, create a believable visionary story, then over time, to build an appropriate, if not, highly competitive, "relationship" (the fundraiser with the best relationship always wins the philanthropic game, according to best in class, development superstar, Tom Coffman at Duke); but then, the leader must "ask for the order."

> **And always remember that the human condition, at some level, is equipped with the inherent need to give, and/or pay it forward.**

In addition, ongoing communication with benefactors is critically important. We all have a distinct responsibility to be great stewards of these priceless institutional relationships. As L.L. Bean professes, your best customer is your last customer.

The final piece of the University of Maine puzzle would have to be the internal family dynamics. Utilizing Dean Stuck's theory per identifying who shapes and influences an organization from an external viewpoint is powerful; however, to institute a long-lasting paradigm shift at a conservative, rather parochial institution with a traditional culture like UM's, you'll need the assistance of insiders with "big juice" to move the masses. At Maine, the university had two "gold plated" treasures: Walter Abbott and Dr. John Winkin.

Walter Abbott was a career Mainer, professor of outdoor studies and experiences, former head football coach, interim director of athletics, the Daniel Boone of Maine, a truly great human being, and an *enormous* "change agent" at UM. As far as Mainers were concerned, Walter had more influence than Jesus at the Last Supper! That said, I suspect Walter never fully appreciated his level of influence—that was just his humble nature. During my tenure, the needle never would have moved without Walter's unqualified support.

The other internal influencer was Dr. John Winkin, who was not only an ambassador of all things Maine, but also an institution within college baseball. A proud Duke graduate from New Jersey, John continually shocked the collegiate community with Maine Baseball's grand exploits—especially post-season. John was the AD and baseball coach at Colby College before his appointment in Orono. Therefore, he was a major asset both inside and outside of the university. John's five decades of service to higher education naturally equipped him with a sense of how the agenda must always be recalibrated to advance the greater institutional mission. Indeed, yet another incredible treasure. During my Maine tenure, both Hickey and Stuck loomed large theoretically; however, practically speaking, Dale Lick, Tom Aceto, Wallace, Davis, Daniel Boone, and "The Coach" really moved the pile, as they say.

To simply characterize Dale Lick—the UMaine president who courageously hired me—as a contemporary leader who was inordinately empathetic and focused on excellence would be most befitting. As I enjoyed a front row seat to Dale's extraordinary vision and supreme purpose, I was indeed provided with both inspiration and a framework relative to what we could emulate within the athletics sector. Dale Lick had an enormous impact on not only my leadership development, but also on the long-term residual growth I enjoyed as a leader over the next three decades.

During my time at UMaine, Dale enjoyed tremendous success in building supreme leaders within higher education. As a renowned "leader's leader," he had five VPs go on to become college or university presidents: Tom Aceto, John Halstead, John Hitt, Greg Brown, Edward Laverty, and Julia Watkins. It is via Dale that I became infatuated with the art of mentoring, if not the human sanctity that it represents.

Needless to say, Jane and I will always savor our special days up in the great state of Maine, as well as our highly impactful relationships with Dale Lick, Tom Aceto, John Winkin, Walter Abbott, Harold Alfond, Larry Mahaney, and all of the amazing coaches, selfless staffers, and dedicated Black Bear student-athletes.

CHAPTER 6

TULANE UNIVERSITY: POLITICAL CULTURE

"They're not your friends."

EAMON KELLY

Just as we were acclimating to the deep, snowy woods of Maine, we received a call in 1991 asking us if we would have an interest in transitioning to serve as the director of athletics at Tulane University. At that point of contact, we knew very little about New Orleans; I had only been there once for a Final Four, and we did not know anyone at Tulane. Paul Tulane, the founder of the university, hailed from Saddle River, New Jersey, which brought a confluence of the northeast to the Deep South, which is alive and well today. For our family, it didn't take long to catch the vibe of this world class city, with all of its lore and uniqueness. The authentic warmth of New Orleanians captured our hearts instantly.

Upon accepting an interview, I began to do some research and discovered that the well-seasoned president, Dr. Eamon Kelly, was from the Bronx, had attended Fordham University, and was ethnically Irish. Moreover,

Eamon was a lifelong friend of Jack Powers, who I knew from Manhattan College, the NIT, and NACDA. In speaking to Jackie Powers, I quickly understood that Eamon was truly Fordham smart, Bronx tough, and Celtically-gifted politically. To be honest, that appraisal proved to be a serious understatement. Eamon Kelly was like the Bono of American higher education, which accounted for his lofty position as a leader of the esteemed Association of American Universities (AAU).

My interview took place in Eamon's office with then board chair, Bob Boh, a long-standing roadway construction giant. There was little room for small talk; Eamon and Bob were terribly straightforward—they were looking for a leader to improve the competitiveness of the athletics program, maintain Tulane's strong academic reputation, raise badly needed resources, and operate a clean program. Just two years earlier, the university had been hit with the John "Hot Rod" Williams point-shaving scandal, which resulted in the suspension of men's basketball for a year.

To be clear, Chet Gladchuk was hired a year earlier to reinstate the program and hire a coach. Chet is an outstanding director of athletics and did all the requisite things needed to bring the program back, as well as secure a tremendous coach in Perry Clark. Perry had been a highly successful assistant at Georgia Tech under Bobby Cremins. So, when I arrived in 1991, having left my cross-country skis and snow shovel in Orono, Tulane was still recovering from the scandal.

As I look back now, it occurs to me that we inherited sizable compliance issues and toxic circumstances in each of the four schools I served in the later years of my career. At Tulane, there was the Hot Rod Williams situation, resulting in a one-year basketball suspension. Five years later, at ASU, I arrived in the ninth inning of the Stevin "Hedake" Smith scandal, which required booking a lot of time early-on with the FBI and the NCAA enforcement team. At Notre Dame, I arrived just as the major violation involving Kim Dunbar providing extra benefits to student-athletes was buttoning up. And finally, I transitioned to Duke amid the conclusion of the infamous Duke Lacrosse travesty.

> **Unbeknownst to me, I had become the "Mr. Clean" of college sports—the go-to AD should a school have a mess in need of tidying.**

Despite the scandal awaiting me upon arrival, I could not have been more excited when I was offered the job at Tulane. Heading down to New Orleans was an adventure—I went first, followed by Jane with five wide-eyed kids (including a newborn) and two dogs all tucked into a Pontiac station wagon with wood paneling on the sides right out of the movie *Vacation*!

1991: The White family begins a new chapter in New Orleans as Kevin White takes on the role of Athletic Director at Tulane University, serving in this capacity from 1991 to 1996.

On the way to the Wilson Center for the press conference wherein my new assignment would be announced, a colleague asked if I had seen that morning's sports section of *USA Today*. Sure enough, the lead story claimed that Kent McWilliams—a.k.a. Mr. Mc (*pronounced Mr. Mack*), former chair of the Tulane Board of Trustees and Tulane's chair of the Athletic Affairs Committee of the Board when I was hired—resigned over my appointment. Kent McWilliams, who was a founding principle at Freeport McMoRan, the only Fortune 500 Company in New Orleans and the greater state of Louisiana at the time, originally wanted an internal candidate to be selected for the role of AD. After doing his homework on me, he felt that I was a NY liberal Catholic, and he was personally offended that I was being hired at his alma mater in the Deep South. Not exactly the launch we had expected.

Most fortunately, in my first year at Tulane, the men's basketball coach, Perry Clark—who'd only been coaching there for a year—was rapidly moving the needle on success. He led the team into five post-season tournaments in a row—historic for Tulane! His non-traditional personality and demeanor electrified New Orleans, which had a superb impact on recruiting and player development—both athletically and academically—and the school's national brand was elevated to heights it had not experienced until more recently. Tulane is a very tough place in which to compete at a top level, yet Perry artfully facilitated the impossible! It was the Camelot period of Tulane Basketball.

At the end of the season, I campaigned aggressively to improve Perry's contract, and somehow won over Mr. Mc in the process! Miraculously, Kent McWilliams came around to me and ended up making several seven-figure gifts to Tulane Athletics over my tenure. Mr. Mc periodically invited me to his impressive hobby farm on the other side of Lake Pontchartrain. We would fish on his lush property (where the pond was well stocked), or simply drive around the farm on a golf cart, drinking a beer or two while we envisioned what a competitive, financially healthy Tulane Athletics program might look like some day. With the renewed financial support of Mr. Mc, who was clearly the top benefactor of Tulane Athletics, we were able to make a good number of much needed financial investments.

Then, of course, there was the Great Gatsby from Montgomery, Alabama— Jim Wilson. Jim served on the Tulane Board, as well as on the Athletics

Committee. Most generously, he always placed his checkbook up on the table to advance the mission of Tulane Athletics.

Way back in the mid-'90s, Tulane Athletics was seriously struggling financially, and the faculty was astir, looking to either downsize or drop athletics altogether. Jim called for an encampment, whereby he marshalled all of the major supporters to his beach house in Destin, Florida. When Jim sounded the siren, all "the players" reworked their schedules and attended.

We sat on Jim's back porch into the early morning while Jim peppered the attendees to ante up. When Jim eventually allowed his guests to retire, the gross pledge amassed over $9M. An amazing amount of resources were raised with little to no notice. For years, all of Tulane referred to that event and the resources raised as the night that the "stabilization fund" was born! It became such a part of the Tulane lore to the point that the immediate community came to think that this was an ongoing practice within broader college athletics.

Jim Wilson loved Tulane. He originally attended Alabama, and for whatever reason, he transferred. Jim was a high-quality center, who became a favorite son of the Green Wave. He had a large hunting property up in Auburn, Alabama, where he would host the biggest decision makers for amazing weekend retreats rooted in camaraderie, southern hospitality, and charisma. Late night conversations with Jim often turned into questions about how a guy from Montgomery could become such good friends with a liberal New York Catholic; he was aghast by that remote reality. Our relationship was inordinately special, for it went further and deeper than with other alums, board members, or employees.

Another, one of many, heralded Tulane supporters was Ben Weiner. Ben, a lifetime bachelor who was affectionately referred to as Uncle Benny, lived in the Fairmont Hotel for fifty years. Uncle Benny was the first mover in the rental furniture business—Weiner Cort—and he amassed his wealth early in his life. Not long after I accepted the ASU AD position and was set to leave Tulane, Uncle Benny summoned me to the Fairmont for our typical room-service lunch of cheeseburgers. As we said our goodbyes, Uncle Benny wanted to gift his estate (in full) to Tulane Athletics, which he did via his lawyer. With regard to philanthropy, authentic relationships really matter. As Tom Coffman, the philanthropic guru at Duke, often says, "Whoever has the best relationship wins the gift at the end of the day!"

We had a very talented athletic administrative team working to facilitate these relationships: Sandy Barbour (became AD at Tulane, California, and Penn State), Ian McCaw (became AD at Northeastern, Massachusetts, Baylor, and Liberty), Jim Sterk (became AD at Portland State, Washington State, San Diego State, Missouri, and Western Washington), Scott Devine (became AD at St. Mary's in Maryland), plus many other major contributors. And on the coaching side, the talent was ridiculously stellar with Greg Davis, followed by Buddy Teevens (football), Perry Clark (basketball, including five post-season tournaments), Lisa Stockton (women's basketball, served a tremendously successful thirty-year tenure), Rick Jones (baseball, unprecedented regular season and postseason success), and so many others.

President Dr. Eamon Kelly was a proud product of the Bronx. He was strong and determined, well equipped politically, scary smart, and not a sufferer of any inhibitions when it came to conveying his mentoring directives explicitly. Late at night, after university functions at the president's magnificent home on Audubon Place, Eamon would often coax me to stay around. Over a night-cap, a quick leadership tutorial might commence.

> To be sure, Eamon always had two quips at the ready: first, "Don't ever get tired!" and second, "They are not your friends!" Eamon would sermonize that his implication here was that all the folks within the respective university beltway who had, at times, oversized opinions on things, did not need to be excessively acknowledged.

For years, throughout my career, following my tenure at Tulane, Eamon's expletive tutoring, as it related to staff exchanges, lived large. Loved Eamon—learned a lot from Dr. Kelly!

Regarding further professional growth at Tulane, I think about how my team—Sandy, Ian, Jim, and I—created a matrix to keep track of the moving parts within the department. We have grown to affectionately refer to the matrix as a three-and-five. Many of us have utilized the matrix throughout our careers, and many others who've come along in later generations not only utilize the matrix in their interview process, but also during their initial press conference. There are so many times when an AD is called upon without warning to bring the senior administration, the board, and/or any group for that matter, up to speed. The three-and-five became a conversational tool devised to simply make sure that we touched all the bases and had our eyes on the ball.

> Within college athletics, there are a lot of moving parts. It is painfully easy to get enthralled with one aspect that does not provide you or your department with a reasonable ROI.

As an example, while working in a high school many decades ago, I worked under a principal (who happened to be a recovering coach) that had an excellent reputation as an educator and leader. This individual often helped the custodial crew break down the tables post lunchtime, jumped up on a ladder to change a burnt-out light bulb, or helped with the landscaping around campus, and he always harvested exceedingly high marks. It took me a few years to fully understand that, while this well intended individual gravitated toward assignments that garnered immediate gratification, no one was doing his primary job of hiring teachers, devising curriculum, evaluating instruction, etc. Consequently, when assessed by our performance standard, we were not a good secondary school. To be honest, we were embarrassingly well below average. (We were damn good at wiping down lunch tables, changing light bulbs, and trimming hedges though.)

It was out this mindset and focus that our administrative team at Tulane collectively identified and created our three-and-five: a list of the three biggest challenges and five best opportunities relative to overseeing college athletics:

BIGGEST CHALLENGES

1. **Balance**—Making sure there is an appropriate balance in terms of time and energy expended between athletics and academics. It is very difficult to maintain the optimum balance in today's entertainment centric environment.

2. **Compliance**—An ongoing tug of war! Over the past several years, college athletics has become very permissive in terms of rules and regulations. Over the history of college athletics, compliance, rules, regulations, and permissiveness have all ebbed and flowed.

> **It takes a lifetime for an institution to garner a brand, and only a nanosecond to burn it to the ground.**

3. **Economics**—Economic reality around college athletics will forever be a supreme challenge. There are never enough resources as the bar is constantly being elevated. The competition to "out do" a rival or peer is never ending. There is so much "funny money" in the system—gimmicky forms of financing, if you will—that it has become increasingly difficult, if not impossible, to compare apples to apples. Most institutions are way outspending their revenue budgets, even considering large university investments. Based on a few former NCAA studies, and then applying what is observable today (anecdotally speaking), I would be surprised if twenty institutions out of a cohort of some 1,100 schools are breaking even. There are so many pieces to this financial puzzle: large student fee investments, state appropriations, tuition waivers, the out-of-state/in-state game, non-billing/charging mechanism within the academy, and the beat goes on…

BEST OPPORTUNITIES

1. **Student Athlete Experience**—The student-athlete experience is critical. Prospective student-athletes today are savvy consumers. They will quickly discern—via direct communication with other gifted kids, or per the rumor mill (social media, ID camps/visits, combines, etc.)—where they will most likely interface with other talented kids. In today's world, an aspirational program must think in terms of not just delivering the experience marketed through the recruiting process, but better yet, over deliver. Kids within this generation inform their respective peers like crazy.

2. **HR**—Your employees warrant your full attention. Division 1 programs spend at least twenty-eight percent of their expense budget on staff (including coaches) salaries and fringe benefits. This is a huge investment in either an incredibly positive marketing mechanism (wherein

coaches and staff support and promote the leader/ pull in the same direction), or the opposite (wherein coaches and staff pull against the leader and operate pejoratively). There are endless ways to communicate and develop staff to be a supreme asset. It's worth the investment of your time and energy!

3. **Politics**—Manage all the competing political forces. There are so many cohorts and constituencies that warrant your attention, and if you do not manage them in an anticipatory way, they will indeed manage you, and eventually engulf you. This opportunity requires ongoing attention, via intellect, energy, and supreme diligence.

4. **Resource Acquisition**—Always near the top of the priority list.

> **Simply put, if you undercapitalize an endeavor, it will either underperform or fail miserably. It is therefore critical that all your revenue streams are fully exploited, including traditional fundraising. Resources matter and must be retained as a big part of the equation.**

Once again, resources must be commensurate with the programmatic objectives or expectations!

5. **Facilities**—Finally, athletic facilities really matter. Prospective student-athletes, matriculating student-athletes, and fans in general (including alums, faculty, staff, and general students) are savvy consumers. Competing in the ever-evolving entertainment world requires an ongoing assessment of facilities. They don't have to be the best, but they need to be representative level facilities!

During my tenure, the prospect of an all sports conference was always top of mind, as well as supreme priority. The most significant interest at Tulane was around joining a football conference. There was some latent seller's remorse still lingering from when Tulane stepped away from the Southeastern Conference (SEC) back in 1965. With no other invitations readily available, joining a conference became a full-time compulsion. There was serious pressure applied by the board of trustees at Tulane to garner an invitation to an existing football conference or, if necessary, create our own. As the ongoing conversation became more real/intense, a group of us secured Chuck Neinas (former Big 12 Commissioner) to support this endeavor. We regularly invited select institutions (Louisville, Memphis, East Carolina, Houston, Southern Miss, USF, SMU, TCU, Tulsa, etc.) who found themselves in a similar circumstance to random meetings at airport hotels in order to discuss how to best create a football conference. Mike Slive, a savvy leader, was also aggressively recruiting those same schools to join his brand-new Great Midwest Conference.

The immediate target list for a new league primarily represented the former Metro Conference institutions that played football, plus a few others. There was significant "push back" via both Louisville and Memphis, for they thought they could remain viable football independents. There were a few others that were sycophantic as well. This ambivalent condition existed for a year or two.

Our charter members were Tulane, Houston, Louisville, Memphis, Cincinnati, and Southern Mississippi. Other non-football playing institutions from the Great Midwest and the former Metro Conference were added early on for scheduling purposes, etc. The wizardry of Chuck Neinas pulled this group into form. However, there continued to be some skepticism among a few of the charter members.

Then, around 1994, there was a National Presidents' Summit in San Diego. I encouraged Eamon Kelly to call a meeting with the above schools and to force the hand of Louisville and Memphis in particular. As a kid from the Bronx, Eamon loved the challenge! In a late-night session in San Diego, he gave his "we need to hang together, or we'll hang separately" speech with I suspect a little NY language and vigor, and he successfully muscled both Louisville and Memphis. They all shook hands and agreed to form what would soon become codified as Conference USA.

Eamon came to my hotel room very late, pounding on the door, to let me know that the "mission was accomplished"! He was beaming! That said, he also disappointingly downloaded (as I had coached Eamon that we needed to hire Mike Slive as the commissioner) that he could not get the group to bite on Mike. So, I pushed Eamon to reassemble the group of presidents in the morning and to be relentless about hiring Mike, for he epitomized the very best option per securing a TV contract and that, not long ago, Mike had successfully launched the Great Midwest Conference. Apparently, Eamon went into the meeting the following morning and pounded on the table. By the time the brunch had adjourned, Mike Slive had been named commissioner. Not sure anybody knows that story within college athletics (including my dear late friend, Mike Slive), for I was the only AD at this National President's summit, operating totally incognito. And thus, Conference USA was born, and Mike Slive would serve as the inaugural Commissioner. As they say, the rest is history.

Mike Slive did a brilliant job as commissioner, along with Chuck Neinas, who we hired as our TV consultant prior to the San Diego summit. The "world class" administrative skills of Mike and Chuck worked together to secure the inaugural TV deal for this brand-new conference. However, it was Eamon Kelly's NY demeanor which created an opportunity for Tulane to paddle forward within this rapidly changing landscape of college athletics.

Jumping Ahead, Chuck Knapp had been the executive vice president for Eamon Kelly before becoming president at University of Georgia, and then search consultant for Heidrick and Struggles. I became close friends with Chuck over the years, with Eamon as the conduit. Therefore, when Chuck Knapp first secured the SEC commissioner search, he traveled to South Bend to spend time with me and noodle about prospective candidates. Of course, I had been hugely impressed with the phenomenal job Mike had done with CUSA; therefore, I made a strong pitch for Mike; I repeatedly told Chuck that Mike Slive was indeed "one-of-a-kind, a truly gifted leader, and a world class politician." Chuck narrowed the search pool down to two or three candidates, then he let me know he was going to enthusiastically push Mike. Of course, I never shared any of this with Mike. The SEC was most fortunate to land Mike Slive, and Chuck Knapp did a great executing/making it happen.

If the number one priority was a conference, the second priority at Tulane was building a basketball venue compatible with major conference association/membership. Whether or not we tried like hell to find a conference to accept us or created our own, a contemporary basketball venue was also thought to be a necessity. It was time to roll up our sleeves again and focus on bringing the donor base together to stabilize the finances and facilities around the Tulane athletic department.

First, we tried to garner financial support for a new arena from the institution with no luck—for the economics were intimidating and Tulane did not have the financial bandwidth. From there, we went to the board chair, Bob Boh, which resulted in the same response. Instead, Bob and Eamon encouraged our team to meet with the mayor of New Orleans, Sydney Barthelemy. Sydney understood our need as I explained that, if we did not find a way to build a facility, Tulane may not find a conference home, putting our Division I sponsorship at risk resulting in an economic loss for the city. Sydney was empathetic and wanted to help. But, sadly, the city of New Orleans was incapable of financially helping.

In turn, Sydney encouraged me to go meet with Louisiana governor, Edwin Edwards. I had a hell of a hard time getting into see Governor Edwards until finally, one of our associate athletic directors, ML Lagarde, mentioned that he knew Edwards—for they occasionally played cards as kids. ML hustled the governor's office and nailed down an appointment for ML and me to meet with Governor Edwards. Again, I made the case for supporting our project—loss of Division I status, loss of potential conference membership, loss of economic impact for NOLA, etc. The governor asked what the total economic loss might actually look like, and I instantly conveyed that it may be as high as "at least $50M per year." The governor, in turn, asked where I got that number, and I freely admitted that we made up the number in the car on the ride up to Baton Rouge.

Believe it or not, the governor sounded supportive, if not positive. He went on to state that if we could produce a legitimate economic impact analysis, and if the figure called for an investment, he would support the prospective project, even though the optics of public money supporting the need of a private institution was not going to be a layup.

Within days of that Baton Rouge summit, I connected with Dr. Tim Ryan at the University of New Orleans, a leading economic impact analyst. Once I laid out for Dr. Ryan what we needed, he was quick to ask, "What was your off-the-cuff estimate that you gave the Governor?" I told him that I said around $50M annually would be at risk without the advent of a facility/venue. To my surprise, Dr. Ryan indicated that my pedestrian analysis was too low, and that he needed two weeks to complete the computations. As it turned out, Dr. Ryan's number was $150M! So, back up to Baton Rouge I went, excited to share the analysis with the governor. He appeared to be pleased and said that if we could get any receptivity within the legislature, and if the bill found its way to his desk, he would sign it.

We had our marching orders! As we made our way through the halls of the capital, it quickly appeared to me that the receptivity toward ML Lagarde was far more favorable than toward this displaced New Yorker. Given that, I asked ML to move into the hotel across from the capital—he would stay there a couple of days a week for eighteen months. Under strict orders, ML lived on one buffet meal a day, for we were running on fumes. In the end, ML's New Orleanian background and charisma carried the day, and Governor Edwards kept his word.

If I remember correctly, the Smoothie King Center cost around $124M to build. Although Tulane eventually went in an alternate direction, the economic impact promise came to fruition via the NBA—today, the arena is the home of the New Orleans Pelicans. Last October, while giving a talk at Tulane, I suggested that, with all due respect to Smoothie King, this "world class" venue should be named the ML Lagarde Center.

Another core element of our time in New Orleans was Toulouse Street, where O'Flaherty's Irish Channel Pub was located. Not only was this the go-to gathering place for our friends and extended family, but during my five years at Tulane, I also did 250 radio shows from the courtyard in back. The proprietor and master musician, Danny O'Flaherty (via the Aran Islands) is a highly valued friend, and a brilliant traditional Irish music talent, even after all these many years. My show was broadcasted on WWL New Orleans from the courtyard out back while someone at the station connected callers to me. The most notable evening was when I had a call-in from "Willie" down in Chalmette, LA. As the infamous story goes, Willie, with his tremendous Cajun accent, called to ask me about the lackluster football season at LSU (Louisiana State University).

Repeatedly, I tried to convey that I was the Tulane guy: "Willie, you should speak with my counterpart at LSU, Joe Dean." (Who, by the way, was an excellent AD!) But Willie would not listen to me—he just kept talking about the Tigers' lack of on-field success. Then, out of the blue, Willie changed gears and wanted insight on the reported LSU NCAA violations. Again, I told him I could not comment on another school. In a huff, Willie closed out the call exchange by declaring: "Well, I don know bout how Curley Hallman runnin' things now, but at least when we was cheatin—we was winnin!" This exchange between a lame duck, courtyard marooned, radio guy (me) and Willie, was drive-time fodder for a heck of a long time.

Kevin White accepting a dare to pet an LSU benefactor's beloved pet tiger.

My final contribution to Tulane would have to be my "last supper" meeting with Big Jim Wilson. Late in my Notre Dame tenure, I received a call from a mutual friend, Sam Scelfo (Tulane alum, former football player). Sam intimated that, earlier that day, he spoke with Jim, and he was beginning to fail quickly. In fact, Jim asked Sam to call me and let me know that, if at all possible, he'd like to see me.

Within a day or two, I jumped on a flight to Montgomery. In his weakened state, Jim personally picked me up at the airport, which surprised me. We went to lunch at the country club he built and owned; Jim had actually *built* the entire high-end subdivision which I had visited several times before. The dining room was empty, not another soul to interrupt us. Jim had requested total exclusivity, barring the four waitstaff overseeing us. The scene, as I reflect, was terribly sobering. Jim recanted his life—the ups, the downs, and the sideways.

After about a half hour, the Great Gatsby of Montgomery grabbed my hand without warning and guided me around his torso which was latent with large tumors—an unspoken message that his end was near. As in the past, he questioned how the hell a New York Catholic liberal and a southerner from Montgomery could have clicked. Again, as I reference throughout this book, life (especially with regard to leadership and philanthropy) is all about relationships. To that end, I learned a great deal from Jim and his best friend, Winona, and their precious family. That goodbye luncheon, where neither of us touched our food, holds a distinctive place in time for me. It was an honor to be Big Jim's close friend, and it was remarkable to be invited to that proverbial Last Supper!

> **At Tulane, I learned about Bronx grit, the power of relationships, and the value of enhancing your network.**

These days, as Tulane has reinvented themselves athletically and built a football stadium on campus, the program is vibrant and competitive as hell. Tulane's modern-day success is attributed to several supreme catalysts: Troy Dannon, former director of athletics, and Mike Fitts, president. Both did a brilliant job relative to advancing athletics. However, the key to the dramatic turnaround has been philanthropist and board chair, Doug Hertz.

After a long absence, Jane and I went back to New Orleans in the fall of 2022 for a Hall of Fame event. It's absolutely incredible to see how competitive the entire program has become. Once again, former board chair, Doug Hertz, and former AD, Troy Dannen, along with President Mike Fitts have done an extraordinary job advancing all aspects of Tulane University, especially athletics. All the major benefactors and alums that have passed—

Kent McWilliams, Jim Wilson, Captain Billy Slatten, Uncle Benny Weiner, Gene Newton, along with Eamon Kelly, Terry Terrebone, ML Lagarde, and so many other Tulanians must be proud as they look down on their beloved Tulane from beyond the starry skies above Lake Pontchartrain.

CHAPTER 7

ARIZONA STATE UNIVERSITY: WELFARE OF THE STUDENT-ATHLETE

"May you grow up to be righteous, may you grow up to be true, may you always know the truth and see the lights surrounding you; may you always be courageous, stand upright and be strong; and may you stay forever young"

BOB DYLAN

A rriving in Tempe, the entire environmental aesthetic was foreign to us. We had never lived in the desert, let alone anywhere out west. Driving on wide, freshly paved streets was a new experience. The landscape was so vast, places were so far apart, and there seemed to be so much clean space. Not to mention that the sky-high palm trees, cacti, huge boulders, and mountains all seemed cinematic or not quite real. And the sun—no one can prepare you for the unrelenting brightness of the Arizona sun.

We had just returned from the terribly generous, original "stabilization" encampment in Destin, Florida, hosted by the Great Gatsby of Montgomery, Alabama, Jim Wilson back in the spring of '96 when I was contacted by a search firm requesting my level of interest in the vacant ASU athletics directorship. Personally, I was anticipating major jaw surgery, which would result in a wired shut jaw for an extended period, followed by adding oversized steel braces for several months after the procedure. Within this sea of activity, although I was curious, I remember thinking that the timing was exceedingly complicated (just like every one of our moves, actually). Leaving Tulane post "stabilization" seemed awkward to say the least. And obviously, the notion of transitioning to a new position with a wired jaw was clearly intimidating.

My curiosity ultimately won out. And upon taking the formal interview, I was told that I was a short lister. However, the competition was steep, and I assumed that I wouldn't have to deal with any potential complications/awkwardness. As I best remember, while waiting for the final decision, I received two very generous inquiries—one from Roy Kramer, then Commissioner of the SEC, and the other from Cedric Dempsey, former longtime illustrious AD at ASU's rival, Arizona—asking me if I wanted the job. Both, unsolicited, asked if they could support my candidacy with ASU president, Lattie Coor. This extra boost of confidence caused my competitive instincts to "kick in," and I encouraged them to help me find the end zone, which they did.

Truth be told, once I wrapped my head around it, I was in oxygen debt relative to this prospect. ASU still had the new-car smell, and it was growing fast! There were around 50K students then, and now there are about 100K students across multiple campuses. Then, there was the Pac-10. Even considering our advent of Conference USA, I was about to be the new AD in the Pac-10!

Not until the press conference announcing my hiring, did I begin to have a complete understanding of the alleged point-shaving scandal that occurred during the 1993-94 season involving Stevin "Hedake" Smith and Isaac Burton. According to historical documentation, there was an arrangement between a local principle and two ASU basketball players that said the players would shave points in end-of-season games in exchange for $250K. However, during one of the games in question, Hedake actually played very well, and the agreement was not satisfied. This enraged the principle! Reports say that the Vegas bookmakers caught on to the scheme because too many people had been coming to town to bet absurdly copious amounts on ASU basketball games.

Naturally, this signaled wrongdoing to both the FBI and the NCAA. Consequently, as the brand-new incoming AD (once again, Mr. Clean), I found myself spending considerable time with both the FBI Investigative Team and the NCAA Infractions Committee until each respective process was fully adjudicated.

The principle, who I believe resided in Paradise Valley (near Tempe), was issued a "disassociation (from ASU) sanction." The "disassociation" was an NCAA term and process utilized regularly for bad actors, and of course I was going to enforce/uphold it. Not long after, there existed "white noise" within the community suggesting that the assertive, new AD had offended the principle and select associates. They were terribly angry at me concerning my call for NCAA disassociation and insinuated that I should "be careful."

Suspiciously, not long after this veiled threat, my late Uncle "Big John" Perretti, along with my aunt Annabelle, came to visit us in Tempe. We were thrilled to see them, but it was out of the blue, and they had never just showed up to visit us before at any of our other homes. Typically, we would visit them at their home on Long Island. It was also a hectic time navigating the new job at ASU, kids in new schools, etc.

John and Annabelle (my father's sister) were the last two unmarried residents in the Honeymooner's sitcom six-floor Brooklyn walk-up. After they married, Big John became a hugely successful contractor on Long Island, winning contracts galore to build schools, hospital additions, municipal buildings, and an array of commercial buildings. As a teenager and beyond,

Kevin and Jane White with Kevin's beloved Uncle John and Aunt Annabelle Perretti.

I worked on many of these select construction projects, wherein I would always be introduced, most affectionately, as Uncle John's favorite *Irish* nephew, never to be confused with the other variety.

The Perrettis stayed in the Valley of the Sun for about two weeks. The first week, they boarded with our family in South Tempe. Then, for the second week, Uncle John and Aunt Annabelle conveyed that they had business in Paradise Valley, and wondered if we could get them a suite at the Arizona Biltmore until they returned to New York. Meanwhile, *The Arizona Republic* news reports were flying about Sammy the Bull's recent relocation from NY to Paradise Valley, along with other members of Uncle John's former New York contingent.

Although we never mentioned a word about the ASU point-shaving scandal or the "white noise" to Uncle John, I have always privately conjectured that Big John Perretti may have heard some angst about his wife's family out in Arizona, whereby his retort to the agitators was to simply stand down. To that end, as Uncle John and Aunt Annabelle flew back east, our Paradise Valley migraine quickly dissipated. That was it; no more noise. Of course, we will never know for sure how things unfolded. However, I do believe that my Uncle John negotiated a hall pass for his favorite Irish nephew.

Moving on to brighter, more welcoming days on campus—almost immediately, en route to my new office overlooking Sun Devil Stadium, I was greeted by both Pat Tillman and Jake Plummer. These two ASU football superstars had carefully compiled a list of student-athlete concerns, and/or "things" that warranted attention if not improvement. To be blunt, I was really impressed and taken aback by their supreme interest in advancing the department. Moreover, their list of articulated concerns extended well beyond their respective sport, Sun Devil Football. Talk about innate, selfless leadership! They ushered me into my office with a yellow legal pad full of all the items inventoried. For the next four years, I kept that same piece of paper in the top drawer of my desk and used it as a quick benchmark assessment of our progress. It became a solid point of occasional reference, if not reflection. During my first year, Pat became chair of the SAAC (Student Athlete Advisory Council), and the initial agenda drawn up by Pat and Jake assumed the support of the larger bandwidth of the Sun Devil student-athlete community. Those were great days, whereby discernible progress was ever-present, largely because of the self-appointed leadership roles taken on by both Pat and Jake.

In the fall of '96, ASU Football was suffering mightily. The Sun Devils had a terrific staff and a well-seasoned coach in Bruce Snyder, but ASU had not gone to a bowl game since the 1987 Freedom Bowl, and that made the ASU faithful vocally skittish. Then, as destiny would have it, Bruce Snyder and company—along with Jake, Pat, and many others—shocked the college football world by running the regular season table, going eleven and zero, ultimately earning an appearance at the Rose Bowl vs. Ohio State.

The superb exploits of the '96 season were many, and they have been well dissected. For me, I will long remember how Bruce Snyder remained inordinately focused, and how the team's leadership subscribed to his earnest belief and superior preparation system. To be sure, one of the greatest turnarounds in college football history fell slightly short of winning the national championship at the 1997 Rose Bowl. ASU took the lead with 1min 42sec on the clock, scoring a touchdown to lead 17-14. Then, with like nineteen seconds remaining in the fourth period, Ohio State's walk-on quarterback, Joe Germaine, who happened to hail from none other than Mesa, Arizona, drove down the field for a touchdown placing the final nail in the coffin. Adding to the intrigue, John Cooper, Ohio State's Head Coach, had been the ASU Head Coach prior to Bruce Snyder. John Cooper had invited Joe Germaine to OSU, which allowed him to eclipse the ASU fourth-quarter lead to win the highly coveted National Championship. ASU ended up finishing fourth nationally. It was a crazy turn of events for an outstanding Sun Devil football team who came within a whisker of winning a national championship. During that storied season, This supreme accomplishment was led by a great coach, the late Bruce Snyder, and a few phenomenal stalwart players, such as: Jake the Snake Plummer, the mighty Pat Tillman, and many others. ASU had not gone to a Bowl Game in eight years, and the program was embroiled in witness protection, under suffocating negativity. That said, all the ASU programs were on a significant upswing, as the Director's Cup would indeed suggest, for in 2000, the university enjoyed a top ten finish.

My tenure at ASU was truly special. So much so that, when I was offered another high-profile Pac-10 AD position as well as recruited to be one of three preferred candidates at a pinnacle Big 10 institution, our personal investment in ASU Athletics remained strong. Upon discussing each opportunity with President Lattie Coor, Jane and I concluded that we were indeed infatuated with ASU and our lifestyle in South Tempe.

> It was never lost on us that we worked with and for a tremendous leader in Dr. Lattie Coor, as well as a group of highly passionate supporters. Our future in Arizona seemed limitless! Without question, my professional growth needle continued to move while we were out in the desert.

The year after my arrival, in the spring of 1997, ASU made a men's basketball change. Bill Frieder was separated from ASU, and we appointed an interim, one of Bill's assistants, Don Newman. Don enjoyed considerable success. However, ASU was looking to reframe the leadership paradigm within men's basketball. After searching long and hard, ASU settled on Rob Evans.

Rob had coached our point-guard son, Mike White, for three years at Ole Miss. Some said Rob's hiring marked the longest interview process in NCAA men's basketball history. That said, for obvious reasons, we needed a damn good basketball coach that could enact a serious cultural change. To be sure, we were looking for a Wyatt Earp prototype to build a barbed wire fence around the program, and Rob had just taken Ole Miss to unprecedented heights competitively. So, although we were not excited about disrupting my son's collegiate experience, we felt that Rob was the perfect fit—which he was indeed! Not long after his hiring, ASU men's basketball out of the rough and profoundly back onto the fairway.

Incidentally, both Newman and Evans were African American, and they were the first high-profile, ethnic minority head coaches hired at ASU, as well as within the State of Arizona. In terms of other key staffers and coaches: Herman Frazier was a longtime ASU athletics administrator, former All American at ASU, and an Olympic gold medalist. In retrospect, Herman would have unequivocally been my pick for AD back in the spring of '96. Herman went on to become the AD at Hawaii and the University of Alabama Birmingham (UAB), before settling into the esteemed number two position at Syracuse. Vic Cegles, a brilliant resource acquisition and development administrator, became the AD at Long Beach State, while Tom Collins, who ran the nuts and bolts of the internal operation, became the AD at Ball State. Following the intense FBI/NCAA point shaving incident, our high-profile external hire was Betsy Mosher, the recovering NCAA enforcement representative, who had previously served as the senior associate AD for compliance at Northwestern. ASU also had an incredibly talented coaching staff back in the day: Linda Vollstedt, women's golf; Charli Turner-Thorne, women's basketball; Sheila McInerney, women's tennis; Pat Murphy, baseball; and Greg Kraft, men's and women's track and field. Combined, this group won innumerable championships—both Pac-10 and NCAA.

During my time at ASU, in the early days of conference realignment, it was first unearthed that amortizing more resources across fewer units was indeed the wave of the future. James Michener—in his 1976 book, *Sport in America*—prognosticated that traditional conferences would become glorified consortiums, only used to negotiate large broadcast property agreements, conduct championships, and arrange the scheduling apparatus. Over time, he argued, rivalries and geography would matter far less. In terms of conference alignment in 1998, the Pac-10 commissioner, Tom Hansen, along with the conference presidents, asked me to speak with Colorado, and asked Peter Dallas, the longtime director of athletics at UCLA, to speak with Texas. The directive was straightforward: if either one, but not both, wanted to join the Pac-10, the conference would issue a formal invitation. Colorado was all in, but Texas balked. The Pac-10 then reversed their position, whereby they would only expand if they could harvest both institutions. This has become an invaluable lesson for me, as I had to communicate to Colorado that my initial communication was indeed disingenuous. It was imprudent to have allowed myself to be in that position, especially with no power over the situation—it was embarrassing as hell, to say the least.

Another ancillary item percolating was within the Pac-10 TV Committee. As a member of this committee, the opportunity to interact with all the players in the broadcast property industry was priceless! Most notably, it helped to facilitate my thirty-year cherished friendship with former ESPN president, George Bodenheimer. My time in the Pac-10 influenced a number of futuristic ESPN TV negotiations to come, including several deals with NBC while I was at Notre Dame.

> **Within sport, particularly college athletics, broadcast property negotiations are akin to facility refurbishment and construction: there is simply no finish line!**

Serving as interim chair of the Pac-10 Men's Basketball Committee during my early days in Tempe is also an experience I continue to savor. As I recall, the rotational chair had to step away. After which I was invited to step into the assignment. Of course, Lute Olson (Arizona) and Mike Montgomery (Stanford) heavily influenced all of the discussions. However, I secretly loved that four former NCBT head coaches from my Loras days were in the Pac-10 mix as well: Ben Braun, California (via Siena Heights); Eddie Payne, Oregon State (via Belmont Abby); Kevin Eastman, Washington State (via Belmont Abby); and Kevin O'Neil, at both Arizona and USC (via Marycrest).

> **This was all a pertinent reminder that many staffers and coaches, including myself, had found a way to become upwardly mobile within the annals of college athletics despite humble beginnings.**

Lastly, and I think about it daily, as my 1997 Rose Bowl watch is the only logo-ed item I still regularly wear. The Sun Devils transitioned from Siberia to West Palm Beach over the course of that undefeated regular season, before being tripped up by Ohio State. My other prized ASU remembrance is a gift from Father Monk Malloy. As I'm sure you are aware, Pat Tillman gave up his pro football career following the tragic events of 9/11 to enlist in the Army Rangers, whereby he devastatingly paid the ultimate price for our country. Upon returning from Pat Tillman's memorial service out in San Jose, Father Malloy gifted us a beautifully framed, enlarged portrait of Pat on the cover of *Sports Illustrated*, which proudly hangs on the wall of my workout room in the house.

Finally, when I need to inoculate myself with the spirit of Pat Tillman, if not the encapsulating ambiance of that adolescent institution of higher learning out in the desert, I think about when our son, Mike White, was invited to Utah Jazz summer camp in Salt Lake City. The *Arizona Republic* ran a brief story about Mike's invitation, and Pat Tillman, unbeknownst to me, got a hold of Mike's phone number. Pat called to berate Mike. He told him that he could not go into that camp opportunity non-competitively, as a non-drafted member of the summer league team; if so, he would regret it. There may have been some explicit language involved within this private conversation, but that was Pat—he was an instigator in the absolute best sense of the word.

We all have people and places that we will never forget—positive experiences as well as less than positive life markers. When we take a step back, they all become part of our human collage, and my ASU collage continues to live very large!

CHAPTER 8

NOTRE DAME: PLURALISM AND POLITICAL CHALLENGES

"The world is more malleable than you think, and it's waiting for you to hammer it into shape"

BONO

The first time I feasted my eyes on the University of Notre Dame was as a coach at Central Michigan University in the fall of 1977. Experiencing the drive onto campus put my chest into a tight holding pattern that I'm not sure I'll ever come out of. Anticipation meets over the top reality when one first sees the main administration building with Our Lady topping it in gold. Without turning your head, in the same frame, sits the glorious Basilica ascending ever higher toward Heaven. The Notre Dame Basilica is not your average campus chapel or Newman Center; it is at least the most beautiful Catholic church in the Midwest. Behind the Basilica, the Grotto of Our Lady of Lourdes opens like an altar out of old-world boulders and stones. Students, faculty, families, and visitors from all over the world visit this sacred place to light a candle and say a prayer to Our Lady. Just breathing the air on campus makes any Catholic feel proud.

KEVIN M. WHITE, Ph.D.

It seems like just days ago that I was happily enjoying our tenure at Arizona State University—then imagine my shock to hear from Gene Corrigan, on behalf of the University of Notre Dame President, Father Monk Malloy. Conveying our supreme interest to Lattie Coor was difficult, if not agonizing, for we thought we'd be lifers in South Tempe. To be frank, we were seriously infatuated with Arizona State and had, in recent months, explained to a few high-profile suiters that we were not movable. The place still had a new car smell, and we were in the right space as far as being the leader and managing the (once again) competing political interests. Both of which were largely due to the staunch support, if not unqualified sponsorship, of Dr. Coor. Yet, when Gene Corrigan, former Notre Dame and Virginia AD, then most recently retired Commissioner of the ACC, cold-called me in late February of 2000 about the Notre Dame opening, I was unexpectedly euphoric; for an Irish Catholic kid from New York to even be considered was quite an honor. We could not have been more settled or deliriously happy at this adolescent school out in the desert, but remember, as a kid, I was indeed a prized employee of the Shamrock Dry Cleaning enterprise! And now, I was being called home to the Irish catholic motherland!

During my first tenure as Director of Athletics at Loras College, I would reach out to Gene Corrigan (former Athletic Director at ND) on a regular basis for endorsement, guidance, and advice; this valuable mentorship and close friendship lasted throughout my entire career. Then later, while at Tulane, I visited Notre Dame once again to meet with Dick Rosenthal (ND Director of Athletics at the time) to discuss scheduling, and then those conversations would spill over into where college athletics was trending. At the risk of being taken as a nut job, I couldn't stop myself from nagging and wearing out my advisors. However, just as Eamon Kelly would say, "Don't Get Tired!" I revered Notre Dame as the pinnacle combination of athletics and academics, coupled with an Irish-Catholic culture that is terribly compatible with my ancestral beginnings.

> **Wherever my path led me, I found myself striving to become a good servant leader. For me, as I progressed, this meant that I had to learn to embody what I strongly believe to be, once again, the four essential characteristics of an effective leader: 1) inordinately empathetic 2) task oriented 3) adaptable, situational, and flexible 4) passionate, if not fairly intense.**

Beginning in my good old Amityville days, rooted in my parents' influence, this ongoing curriculum somehow presented itself only to be re-enforced innumerable times along this long and winding road. That said, I never imagined that I would ever be lucky enough to be a leader at the University of Notre Dame. As the late Don Keough, former ND Board chair, would often quip, to really know/understand Notre Dame, you'd have to "hear the music." Well, instantly, we heard the music, and to be sure, some twenty-four years later, we still hear the music!

Serving as the Director of Athletics at Notre Dame from 2000 to 2008 was a blessing to not only Jane and me, but to our whole family. Of course, despite my best intentions, intense personal analysis has garnered the outplay that I failed on the biggest stage of my career per being the consummate leader. At the end of the day, I did not manage the competing political systems effectively, and as you may glean from previous chapters, I *knew* better. As I reflect on our eight years in South Bend, either in the still of pre-daylight on a run, or late at night looking into the woods from our porch in Durham—it is within a sort of dark, sober space that I tend to revisit my Notre Dame tenure quite regularly, which now dates back some sixteen years. It bears repeating that the highly instinctive capacity

Kevin White is named Athletic Director at Notre Dame University in Indiana, serving from 2000 to 2008.

to always be able to read the room and to be exceedingly anticipatory is an invaluable skill, particularly within the required "skill set" that begets athletics administration as well as coaching, for college athletics is simply a "people on people" relationship-driven enterprise. To this point, it is also important to note that every interpersonal exchange is filtered through the bassinet from which one came from, along with one's various life exposures and unique experiences; there is a primary, foundational point of view that galvanizes one's heart, private thoughts, and intentions. The truth is that it can never be assumed or taken for granted that anyone is on the same page regarding anything.

Given that, as I have stepped away from my thirty-eight year tenure as a Director of Athletics just three years ago, it has become even more abundantly clear to me that an AD within this moment in time can indeed delegate all other day-to-day functions, to some degree, flashing in and out of those respective topical disciplines (e.g., development, compliance, student-athlete services, academics, facilities, both internal and external operations, etc.); however,

> the AD must be the leader (be the face, the voice, provide the vision, and basically conduct the symphony).

The other area that can't be delegated is managing daily communication, including all political forces, wherein oftentimes they are competing forces. As I privately reflect on my time at Notre Dame, those two responsibilities were unequivocally under-attended. The unique dynamic that shapes the University of Notre Dame is that there are a number of different constituencies, many of which love the place perhaps too much. Objectivity becomes muted by emotion. A simple diagnostic tool that I have long used to assess a wide variety of situations is "I over E," which is my shorthand for "Intellect over Emotion." However, the emotionally charged Notre Dame community often proved impervious to logic. It is the most powerful catholic school on the planet; the Board of Trustees, mass media, and alumni base all compete for influence. As for my era, I could have done a better job of managing those competing, emotionally based perspectives. After sixteen years (removed), I accept and acknowledge that it was my responsibility to control the environment to a certain extent and to better apply the elements of Political Theory 101, which I currently preach to my students at Duke's Fuqua School of Business. I cannot say for sure whether someone else might have been more effective in navigating the same set of circumstances at the time.

> One cannot overestimate the tremendous "Art of Anticipation" which has been a conversational theme of mine with staff, specifically within town hall meeting formats. I often find myself expounding upon just how this aspect of personal and professional sustenance became ever-present in my life.

Nostalgically, I recall working as a child (on assorted manual labor projects) with my uncle, James Patrick "Spot" O'Donnell (my mother's brother), wherein I regularly harvested the mini lecture: "If I have to tell you to grab the other end of the object, it's already way too late!"

Also, as a young man, I had the distinct honor of working for another uncle, John Perretti (my father's brother-in-law whom you may recall from the ASU chapter), who owned several commercial construction businesses around Long Island. "Big John Perretti," as he was often called, grew up alongside my father in Jackie Gleason's six-floor walkup in Brooklyn, and later married my father's sister. To be sure, by proper distinction, I became Uncle John's "Irish Nephew," whereby he always found employment for me during the summertime and through the holidays when I was home from college. Uncle John ramrodded me through the union protocol, and I was paid rather handsomely, which continues to be, some fifty-five years later, deeply appreciated. Regardless of the building project, I always had the same job: a "tender." Code here, is that I was charged with providing all the block, brick, and mud (via wheelbarrow) to the brick and block layers so they could most efficiently continue forward uninterruptedly at a swift pace. Of course, a familiar mantra was always in the air on these job sites—"if we have to tell you what to do, or when to provide the necessary supplies, it's already too damn late!" Hence, whenever I found myself behind the curve, I would be the target of what I later termed as "New York language." All the graphic pronouncements, as well as various unique combinations, flew liberally.

Although the "Art of Anticipation" does not appear on any of my formal transcripts, I have always deeply understood the nonnegotiable concept, as well as the respective consequences for not complying in a timely manner. Therefore, I have repeatedly preached this concept with anyone and everyone with whom I have been associated. My kids often say that I lead the nation relative to redundancy, and this particular topic regarding the immense value of anticipation may indeed be my leader in the proverbial clubhouse. My maternal grandmother, Mariah Boyle O'Donnell (Nanny O) was widely considered to be someone who possessed mystical knowledge deep rooted in ancient Celtic culture. Of course, I am not sure that those respective powers don't readily exist within a great many cultures. However, Mariah was looked to for her unique vision, for she could somehow see around the corner (a favorite expression of Duke Emeritus President, Dr. Richard Brodhead). For a very select group of individuals, having the ability to connect with the unseen world is an art form, while it defies explanation. Nanny O would often predict an unanticipated death or an exciting development before it actually occurred and/or could be anticipated. She would say that she was "sensitive to spirits." Moving from art form to science, I might warehouse this activity within the great anticipatory silo. To that end, I have personally, on occasion, felt like I am vulnerable to the "Mariah Zone" when an unexplainable, somewhat magical occurrence grabs my full attention.

Back to the phone call—Gene Corrigan, on behalf of Rev. Edward "Monk" Malloy c.s.c. (then President of Notre Dame), was inquiring whether we would have an interest in the director of athletics position at Notre Dame, and all bets were off. The details were thin, for I understood that they had a short list of four, and that maybe three would be invited for an interview in mid-March, should I want to participate in the process.

Honestly, we felt that it was truly a long shot, at best. Not having been in Tempe for a long time, and not imagining that this could indeed occur, we chose not to mention this expression of interest to anyone, including family, except to Dr. Lattie Coor, ASU President. At that point, our youngest daughter, Mariah (my grandmother's namesake), was nine years old and in the fourth grade. The interview was slated for the Hilton Chicago within the O'Hare Airport, so we arranged for Mariah to stay at a friend's house for the weekend. En route to the airport, we stopped by her school to pick her up and drop her at her friend's house; and as Mariah ran to the car, Jane remembered that she had not submitted an outstanding book report. So, Jane told Mariah that she needed to run back into the school and get a book from the library. *Keep in mind, Mariah had no idea that we were heading to Chicago for an interview or that the Notre Dame job was in the air.* Yet, as Mariah hurried back to the car, she held up a book entitled: *Childhood Stories of Knute Rockne*. Needless to say, we were stunned, within a state of utter shock. That story, along with the Jim Crowley story as told in the first chapter, fits into that "Mariah Zone" of ancient Celtic mysticism. These experiences, as well as many others, serve to reconnect me, if not all of us, to our ancestral bassinet. Despite any regrets I may have about how my time at Notre Dame played out, I cannot ignore the feeling that the signs were all there—leading us to that place. Sometimes we are meant to be somewhere for reasons that are not clear to us. Mariah Boyle O'Donnell, via Falmore, Donegal, Ireland, lives in perpetuity within my mind, heart, and unyielding imagination.

The entire way of life at Notre Dame is eminent. There is a distinct odor of pride in the air. All of its constituencies love the mission, the institutional history, and the traditions well beyond what seems reasonable. It would be tough to find any person on campus or even in the greater South Bend area that does not unflinchingly praise Notre Dame, and it was flattering to be invited into this alluring culture. However, as a non-Notre Dame alum, my instinct was that I was not in a promising position to be selected. Nevertheless, Jane and I flew to O'Hare on March 13 for the interviews, which were scheduled for the following day at the airport's Hilton Hotel.

The interview process was pretty straightforward. Early that afternoon, I spent several hours with select members of the university's administration, coupled with a handful of highly distinguished board members—Andy McKenna, Don Keough, Bob Welsh, among others. At the conclusion of this session, one or two other interviews were scheduled. So, I was asked if we could hang around the hotel for the rest of the day. Later that evening, Father Monk Malloy, Notre Dame's acclaimed president, came to our room, and we had yet another elongated conversation, which ended in an offer. You could have knocked both Jane and I over with a feather. Monk was classic Monk—incredibly gracious and concerned about our level of comfort. We never discussed the salary, although I would have found a way to pay Notre Dame at that point! Upon request, we rendered our ASU contract, whereby ND indicated that they would match it, which they did.

The press conference occurred the next day immediately upon our arrival in South Bend at the main building, announcing a start date of April 14, 2000. A sizeable crowd of Notre Dame administrators, staffers, coaches, etc. showed up with little to no notice, including Joe Piane, who is a longtime friend, yesteryear track coach, colleague, and Loras graduate. Joe and I have been close friends since the mid '70s, and we continue to be great, lifetime confidants. Beyond Joe, I really didn't know many of the other press conference attendees all that well. My mind was swirling with thoughts about my parents and grandparents, for I wished they could have been a part of this incredible moment. The ND attendees could not have been more personable and/or ready to assist us in our transition. Bottom line: we were immediately embraced well beyond what could have been expected. The press conference itself was pretty typical. The questions covered everything from the quick hiring process through to, "Why ND?" For reasons previously noted, responses flowed easily. But not unlike most frenetic transitions, the first several months on the job were absolutely chaotic. There is an ardent desire to be in multiple places, meet all the key and influential players, learn the culture, history, and traditions, all while also meeting the entire staff.

My very first sign that things on the inside were not as they appeared to be on the outside occurred about a month after my arrival when I was summoned to the office of a high-profile board member. Naively, I thought I'd be saluted for a good onboarding effort: I had been running long and hard each and every day. But to my utter surprise, I was lectured, even chastised, for immediately aligning myself (both practically and politically) with the senior administration of the university. The vice principal-type lecture suggested that select board members were highly disappointed in my not reading the environment better, if not much quicker. In hindsight, this was merely a power play to let me know who was really in charge at Notre Dame, and (in their eyes) it was not Rev. Monk Malloy, the president of the university and the man who hired me. I was fresh leadership meat, and they were aggressively recruiting me to align with an alternate power group. Upon returning to campus, and inquiring further, I learned about an apparent organizational schism, which would, unfortunately, underscore most activities/initiatives moving forward.

> **Once again, in many organizations, you will find a formal chain of command and an informal chain of command (as introduced in the Loras chapter); however, my time at Notre Dame taught me how lethal an informal (alternate) power base can be if left unchecked.**

No one is a better leader or human being than Rev. Monk Malloy, and I am proud to say that we aligned professionally, morally, and ethically; it was futile for anyone to try to persuade me to undermine him in any way—not just because I am loyal, but also because Monk and I were of the same mindset.

> **One of my most prideful moments at ND occurred as I listened to Father Monk Malloy provide me with a year-end evaluation: he carefully, candidly, yet also pointedly, conveyed what he characterized to be one of my strongest attributes/strengths which was that he would never wonder what I was really thinking, for he knew that I would always tell him what was in my head and in my heart.**

On the other hand, the board chair (in my early years there) and I never saw eye to eye, and we always had irreconcilable differences. Unfortunately, he was given unqualified bandwidth via a faction of the board with a few Holy Cross Community supporters as well. His biggest supporter, if not influencer, was a rogue priest who had designs on becoming the next president of the university, which fortunately did not come to fruition as he was later dismissed from his ecclesiastical duties. Fundamentally, I did not respect those men; but I wish I could have found a way to manage them better.

The Notre Dame Board of Trustees is very large, particularly when you include emeritus members. It is comprised of major benefactors and influential players that oversee the university administration. In addition, the Holy Cross order has significant (historical and cultural) skin in the game. And there are, not unlike most groups of humans, sub-sects that subscribe to different organizational and/or operational perspectives. This is more typical than not across institutions of higher education. That said, at Notre Dame, the emotional connection and obsession with the public image of Notre Dame takes the possessive mentality of trustees to yet another level when compared to similar boards at other colleges/universities.

As for Father Ned Joyce, Father Ted Hesburgh, Father Jim Riehle, and my great confidant and dear friend, Father Monk Malloy, among so many within the Holy Cross Community, we felt warmly embraced and unconditionally accepted. Most ironically, upon returning to South Bend for Fr. Jim Riehle's funeral shortly after I left for Duke, I had my last in-person conversation with Father Ted Hesburgh (iconic leader who served as president of ND for thirty-five years prior to Father Malloy) next to my rental car immediately following the service. And Father Ted, who was very close to Jane and me, hugged me tightly and said, "Do you know why I love you, Kevin? I will always love you because you keep your mouth shut." My mind raced with thoughts of board meetings that could tarnish the good reputation of Notre Dame. Looking back, I know that Father Ted valued my loyalty to the university, particularly in times when I was under fire and not shown in the best light. However, the University of Notre Dame is bigger than any one of us. To be clear, I had never, nor will I ever go public with the specifics of board room conversations out of love and respect for the university, its numerous high-quality leaders and colleagues, its tremendous student body, and its legacy of outstanding Holy Cross Priests such as: Fr. Ted, Fr. Ned, Fr. Jim, and Fr. Monk Malloy. That said, the aforementioned represents

Kevin with the Fathers at Notre Dame.

the extent of the detail that I am willing to share in that regard, even after all this time.

Father Jim Riehle was, as they say, a supreme piece of work! During select sojourns to Ireland, away games, or at our home over the holidays, Father Jim would bring, as the Irish say, "the craic"! He was the chaplain for the athletics department and was featured in the movie *Rudy*, in which he played himself. Most importantly, Fr. Jim was a close confidant and good friend. I suspect that he saw the entire sitcom unfold, though he never divulged this to me.

Kevin White pictured with Rev. Edward "Monk" Malloy, 16th president of the University of Notre Dame (1987-2005). Kevin regards him as "the most Christ-like human on the planet" and credits Father Malloy with teaching him "level five" leadership.

Via NCAA circles, I knew Father Ned well, and Jane and I were both close at hand (daily) when he eventually passed. Of course, his best friend, Fr. Ted was always "in vigil" as Father Ned slowly slipped away. Their lifelong history of friendship was legendary! They were like Butch Cassidy and the Sundance Kid for well over three decades. It was a legendary bond. Our relationship with Father Ted was also robust; he would often call our home and tell us to drop everything to have dinner with him—it was non-negotiable. As I have often quipped, at the risk of sounding sacrilegious, "If I am ever invited to the 'golden gates' to meet the 'Big Guy,' it will indeed be anticlimactic, for I have already rubbed shoulders with Father Ted at his beloved Notre Dame."

With regard to Monk Malloy, he is the most Christ-like human on the planet. It was from Fr. Malloy that I learned "level five" leadership (as coined by Jim Collins, author of *Good to Great*). He was undeniably mission-centric as a leader, humble to a fault (which is an understatement), self-effacing, as well as highly competent in terms of all the most desirable human characteristics. Jane and I, as well as our family, absolutely loved the Holy Cross community! Over our eight years in South Bend, with Monk's unqualified support, we brought all NCAA programmatic scholarships to full complement, which made Notre Dame Title IX compliant, further enhancing the broad-based prowess of the entire athletics program.

> **Throughout my thirty-eight years as a director of athletics, I can honestly convey that I was afforded the distinct opportunity to persist only because of the tremendous leaders that were on our team.**

Upon reflection, some thirty-two former staffers have become ADs and/or conference commissioners representing something like seventy different institutions. Specifically, from our staff at Notre Dame, the North Carolina "triangle area" is well surrounded. Jim Phillips, the current commissioner of ACC, and all three athletic directors in the triangle today worked with me at Notre Dame: Nina King at Duke, Boo Corrigan at NC State, and Bubba Cunningham at UNC are all from our all-star staff at Notre Dame.

Overall, I feel ridiculously lucky and proud as I reflect upon my 2000-2008 UND staffers who have since emanated into significant leadership roles within the greater intercollegiate athletics landscape: Jim Phillips served as associate director of athletics, and then senior associate director of athletics for external affairs at ND from 2000-2004 (now, commissioner of the ACC), and Bill Scholl was the long time deputy athletics director for development (recently retired VP and AD at Marquette). Bill had tremendous fundraising acumen, which helped us launch an aggressive athletics facility master plan which resulted in the construction and/or redevelopment of a significant number of athletics venues. Scholl was also instrumental in concepting the Shamrock Series, which has become a successful mainstay of the Irish Football program. My successor Jack Swarbrick's stellar leadership (along with deputy AD Missy Conboy and select others) has aggressively advanced all facility projects to the next level.

Other successful team members include Bernard Muir, current AD at Stanford; Sandy Barbour, recently retired AD and VP at Penn State following stints as AD at University of California and Tulane; Bubba Cunningham, now the rockstar AD at UNC and current chair of the NCAA Men's Basketball Committee; Boo Corrigan, AD at North Carolina State and former chair of the College Football Playoff Committee in 2024; Allen Greene, VP and AD at University of Pittsburgh; Nina King, VP and AD at Duke, wherein Nina recently served as chair of the NCAA DI Women's Basketball Committee; Stan Wilcox, current Executive VP of the NCAA; Chris Reynolds, AD at Bradley and former chair of the NCAA DI Men's Basketball Committee; Josh Berlo, VP and AD at University of Denver; Andrew Goodrich, VP and AD at Gardner-Webb University.

To be painfully honest, this legacy makes me (and Jane) exceedingly proud.

> **However, what makes me most proud is that, across that large cohort of appointments, around 30% of the leaders are members of historically underrepresented communities. At all but one of the six schools wherein I served as the director of athletics, we hired the very first Black head coach at the school, and, in several instances, within the state.**

This is what we hold privately as our biggest contribution to the greater enterprise. In addition, as a director of athletics over roughly four decades, I was 100% successful in finding established (or up and coming), talented female coaches to lead women's programs.

Sport is clearly one of the most powerful sociological mediums within both our domestic and global societies. The Civil Rights era in America was heavily influenced by sport, along with the advent of television in the early '50s and '60s. One such historical, pivotal moment took place during the Rome Olympics in 1960, when Wilma Rudolph inspired the entire world as an Olympic Champion. There have been many historical moments wherein sport was an enormous catalyst for changing perceptions surrounding race and gender. And over my professional life, I have developed a compulsory commitment to DEI.

> **Having a fair, if not reasonable, cohort of under-represented individuals within the collegiate athletics framework is critical to the future of the enterprise.**

Back in South Bend, the ebb and flow around our Notre Dame tenure was inevitably tied to the fortunes impacting football. Notre Dame Football enjoys a rich, robust, national tradition and fan base, not to mention its own television network contract with NBC and an access point relative to post season play. Moreover, it is the only collegiate football program with a brand that carries global expectations. To make a long story short, Notre Dame Football has made Notre Dame what it is. Football is the driver of the brand. Financially, football carries all other sports. Ticket sales, ancillary income, premium sales, income from broadcast properties, etc. have created a peerless asset within college athletics.

When I arrived in the spring of 2000, Irish football was suffering from a lack of programmatic momentum. Bob Davie had not long before taken over the reins of the head coaching position from famed coach, Lou Holtz. Most unfortunately, Bob's appointment was not gleefully supported, which tends to quickly marginalize a new leader. So, when I arrived, there was ample chatter surrounding Bob's future. During our first fall, Bob exceeded expectations and had a better-than-expected season. However, just two years later, the greater Notre Dame community began to foreclose on Bob. In my view, Bob was a damn good coach who represented all the intangible qualities of a distinctive leader and respected coach. That said, when the foreclosure process begins, it is ridiculously hard to stop.

In December of 2002, we launched a supreme effort to secure a football coaching successor. Early on, Tyrone Willingham was my choice, and Fr. Monk Malloy's as well. Unfortunately, a pocket of board members pushed back, and we could not harvest any consensus regarding Tyrone. So, the university hired two former high-profile commissioners to aid in our search. In a meeting at the FBO in Cleveland, along with Monk and select board members, we laid out a recruitment and hiring plan. Geographically speaking, we had a former commissioner from the east (Gene Corrigan) to consult, and one from the west (Chuck Neinas). There were a lot of cooks in the kitchen, and for a coach to even be considered at Notre Dame, they had to meet a highly selective non-negotiable list of standards. These restrictive qualifications and guidelines regarding prospects were never just based on my opinion; they were set by the hiring culture. As I best recollect, the qualifications were as follows:

1. Must be committed to academic rigor concerning admissions; recruiting prospects must be top tier student-athletes.

2. Must be committed to the non-negotiable integration of student-athletes with all other students (in terms of dining, housing, etc.).

3. Preferably Catholic; if not, must be committed to the religious environment.

4. Domestic/personal mulligan was a significant speed bump (for example, divorce).

5. Must have an excellent record of compliance/good behavior per their current student-athletes.

6. Must show good academic performance of current student-athletes.

7. Outstanding track record of competing and recruiting success.

8. ND was proudly un-interested in driving upwardly the coaching compensation game. Back then, ND was indeed conservative relative to salaries.

Therein, as best remembered, those factors made the search a supreme challenge, for the pool was exceedingly small, and some desirable prospects were also contractually unavailable. In addition, coaches across the industry were well aware of the internal pressures from the board and the external pressures from the media, not to mention the global magnifying glass they'd be living under as the Notre Dame Football coach. Over time, we whittled our list down to two prioritized/preferred prospects.

As many would remember, we hired George O'Leary. Within our #1 to #8 considerations, he fit quite well. Beyond the obvious matrix, one of our high-profile board members knew George socially and campaigned appropriately for his respective appointment. It mattered more to me that one of

Kevin White cheering on the sidelines of the Notre Dame football field.

our entrusted (highly esteemed) leaders, as well as the former ACC Commissioner, vouched for George like crazy. The quip often used at the time was "George was out of central casting" for the ND Football job. And all of that was true. Beyond that, George was a damn good football coach! Later, he had a brilliant run at UCF, not unlike the run he enjoyed at Georgia Tech.

Alas, as history would note, five days after George's appointment, it was unearthed that his resume was invalid. There was a playing discrepancy, compounded by academic degree inaccuracies. It was a life altering, unrecoverable moment for George and his family. It wasn't easy to be me in the media at that time either, but I empathized with George and hated to see him suffer. It was apparent that he hadn't embellished by design; this cooked-up resume thing just got away from him over many decades, and it was too late for him to rewrite his resume as he had been hired by other schools with the same credentials. To add a little more color to the story, George's bio at previous institutions like Syracuse and Georgia Tech reflected the same inaccuracies. At that time, formal background checks were not as sophisticated as they are today. Unfortunately, the information/ documentation relied on was supported by historical information garnered from the media systems at prior schools where George had been employed. The "college playing history" discrepancy was unearthed by a reporter doing a story on his hire, and once that became public—there was a deeper dive that revealed the graduate degree issue. This very public situation no doubt caused coaches across the country to revisit their own resumes.

In fairness to the situation some twenty-odd years later, it must be noted that ND abides by an unwavering honor code. It would have been impossible to hold matriculating students and staffers to that immaculate standard while not enforcing the same standard on a newly hired head coach. Letting George go was undoubtedly one of the toughest decisions I have ever faced. I'm not sure I handled it correctly, but I am quite sure that I *would* handle it the same way should I ever find myself in that position again.

Obviously, this all required a massive pivot. After things blew up, there weren't many players left hanging around the campfire. Therefore, I (with Monk's blessing) circled back to Tyrone and made the hire. It wasn't difficult for me, as Tyrone had long been my top choice! He had a great tenure at Stanford wherein he was widely heralded as a tremendous talent, particularly upon taking Stanford to the Rose Bowl in 2000 and being adorned with just about every award imaginable, including coach of the year recognition. In addition, with clean hands, I knew Tyrone from my track coaching days at Central Michigan when he was on Roy Kramer's football staff. We coached a few of the same kids who were multi-sport athletes. Then, down the road, when I was the director of athletics at ASU and Tyrone was at Stanford, we reconnected. Therefore, I felt that I knew Tyrone quite well, and relative to these public-facing positions, that becomes a significant factor—particularly following the recent chain of events. I knew that I could trust Tyrone to act with integrity.

After year one, wherein Tyrone won ten games, he was heralded as national coach of the year (per several outlets) and featured in *Sports Illustrated* with the byline: "Return to Glory Notre Dame: What a Difference A Coach Makes."

However, the paradigm shift surrounding Tyrone Willingham cooled when segments of the Notre Dame community, both on and off campus, aggressively turned on him pretty quickly after that first season. Years two and three were met with roadblocks, undermining, and ongoing signs of foreclosure. To be clear, the individual within the sitcom that misread the environment and/or did not onboard Tyrone most effectively was me. I don't think the exit ramp would have been so short circuited if I could have managed it better.

It is widely understood that it takes time for programs to ferment in terms of recruiting, player development, and implementing a new coaching style. Yet, within college football, there persists a cyclical nature of changing coaches without giving them the necessary runway to take off. Specifically, when a school is not winning and raising their program to the level at which they perceive themselves to be (no matter how unrealistic it may be at the time), some constituents will panic and retaliate against the coach. If/when the life cycle of the coach is truncated before reasonable time is allotted, it is also in part because it is based on the later stages of the previous regime's efforts and/or productivity, or lack thereof. Tyrone exemplified all of our qualifications and withstood a pressure-cooker of inflated expectations. He was also working with players who were recruited by someone else entirely—Bob Davie—and he was developing them and winning games. Unfortunately, he could not win enough games for a certain faction of the board. Because when the guy you have is not the guy you want, it is easy to devalue him and make him a scapegoat.

Even with the full support of President Malloy, I was unable to persuade the board to honor Tyrone's contract. Although it clearly wasn't my choice at the end of the day, I must (and do) take full responsibility for Tyrone's short tenure at Notre Dame. Tyrone was my pick, I put him in play, and I didn't do enough to garner more support for him to secure his full tenure. In hindsight, I needed to get more of the politically influential people to buy into Tyrone's appointment on the front end. Because at the end of the day, the political environment proved to be more crucial than performance on the field.

Tyrone Willingham is a great man and a great coach. At the University of Notre Dame in 2001, we hired perhaps the highest profile ethnic minority head coach in the history of college football at a supremely influential university. Most unfortunately, Tyrone was never fully accepted by everyone, which accounts for his premature separation in year three, after being national coach of the year in year one and featured on the cover of *Sports Illustrated* pronouncing his competent, highly transformative leadership. For me, holding the press conference and announcing that we would not be moving forward with Tyrone was the hardest thing I've ever had to do in my career—it was an almost out-of-body experience where it didn't feel like I was saying the words. It was brutally unjust, and Monk and I were both devastated over being unable to stop it.

As I have many times espoused, college athletics is in the leadership development business. We aggressively market a life-changing experience, coupled with a heightened "lifetime" opportunity to the next generation of aspiring student-athletes.

> Therefore, an artificially influenced environment without under-represented leaders, represents a terribly flawed leadership curriculum for all student-athletes—if not for the greater higher education community as well. If we—as athletics administrators, coaches, or citizens at large for that matter—continue to neglect this important responsibility, as Uncle Jimmy and Uncle Johnny would say, it will always be too damn late!

After Tyrone's exit, there was a strong interest in hiring a Notre Dame graduate. The challenge with that objective was that there weren't any hirable alumni prospects currently coaching within college football. Moreover, as best I can remember at that given time, there were only three Fighting Irish alums working within the entire NFL, none of which had been a head coach in either college or the NFL. All leadership styles tend to be a bit different. No better or worse. Just authentically different based on personality and technical pedigree. That said, without prior collegiate head coaching experience, it was difficult to compare and/or contrast candidates across the agreed upon matrix as inventoried previously. And again, the obvious candidates, who would most likely agree to be viable options in the open market, were simply not interested or contractually unavailable.

Therefore, Notre Dame pivoted to three-time New England Patriots Super Bowl champion offensive coordinator, Charlie Weis (ND Alum). And since Charlie had no collegiate coaching experience, there was an expressed interest in securing a collegiately seasoned staff, preferably with coordinators who had previously served as a head college coach. Charlie hired David Cutcliffe, who I knew as well via the Manning family from our time down in New Orleans.

After only a few months, early in the spring of 2003, David faced a serious health issue and had to separate from ND—he returned to Oxford, Mississippi, and then back to Knoxville, Tennessee, to fully recoup. Several years later, I transitioned to the director of athletics role at Duke, upon meeting a contractual obligation to separate from ND for the sum of $1,146,024; therein, David and I spent thirteen years together where he manufactured the very best Duke football run in forty years. Charlie enjoyed early success in part due to Tyrone's successful recruiting classes who ended up being Charlie's juniors and seniors. He then received a ten-year contract extension after year two so as not to fall into the revolving-door of the coach recruitment trap. Charlie strongly appealed to select NFL teams, because he was a damn good strategist.

Through the ups and downs, we loved being at Notre Dame—not unlike every other stop on our lifelong career pathway. Sometimes we underperform or have regrets; however, there are often circumstances that can't be overcome when the timing is just poor.

> **I believe that we can achieve just about anything in life, but we can't always control where and when we achieve it.**

I viewed Notre Dame as the magically, athletically, mystical endpoint (destination) based on my ancestral background. Before I landed there, it was absolutely unachievable in my mind; I had never dreamed about that professional prospect. Notre Dame was peerless, one of one. I thought it was well beyond my reach, and in some ways, it was.

Jack Swarbrick, along with the support of Fr. Jenkins, accomplished great things at Notre Dame. Marcus Freeman was a brilliant football hire; from my vantage point, he meets all of the aspirational characteristics of a highly gifted leader. Niele Ivey, ND's talented and successful women's basketball coach, was named the 2022-23 ACC WBB Coach of the Year! And newly appointed men's basketball coach, Micah Shrewsberry is an exciting addition to Notre Dame's thriving, high profile coaching staff. Notre Dame has distinguished themselves within college athletics by having three outstanding head coaches that just happen to be of ethnic minority within their major programs.

In closing this chapter, let me say that I loved working with all of the outstanding coaches and student-athletes over my eight years at the University of Notre Dame. I have particularly fond memories of working with Muffet McGraw and supporting/witnessing her first NCAA Women's Basketball National Championship in 2001. And I am especially proud of hiring Mike Brey, whose twenty-three-year tenure was utterly amazing—he also continues to be a great friend. Jeff Jackson, who has made Notre Dame Hockey an enduring national power, leading them to several Frozen Fours, is also a highly valued friend. And the highly regarded Notre Dame Lacrosse Coach, Kevin Corrigan, just won his second NCAA Championship in the spring of 2024 continues to be close at hand. Jane and I are over the moon proud to have two Fighting Irish graduates in our family: Danny graduated in 2002 and is now vice president and director of athletics at the University of Tennessee; and Brian graduated in 2006 and is now the vice president and director of athletics at Florida Atlantic University.

Lastly, I would be remiss if I didn't convey that our proudest personal moment at ND occurred at a Monogram Club annual dinner at our home in Shamrock Hills. Held on our side lawn in late May, the Notre Dame Alumni Association hosted some 300-plus attendees and, unbeknownst to us, provided Jane and I with Honorary Alumni Awards. Of all the honorary and material gifts we have received—and we have indeed been spoiled rotten—that day will indeed stand out in perpetuity.

CHAPTER 9

DUKE UNIVERSITY: PHILANTHROPY, RELATIONSHIP AND LEADERSHIP IMPERATIVE

"Make it Matter."

GENERAL MARTIN E. DEMPSEY,
FORMER CHAIRMAN OF THE JOINT CHIEFS OF STAFF

In late May of 2008, my great confidant and mentor, the late ACC commissioner emeritus, Gene Corrigan, contacted me on behalf of Dick Brodhead to inquire whether I might have an interest in transitioning to Duke from Notre Dame. Yes, the same mentor who reached out to me on behalf of Notre Dame eight years prior; as Harry Chapin would say, "All my life's a circle." Gene had lived within both communities: he was a graduate of Duke and had been the longtime ACC commissioner; and in the same breath, he had served as the director of athletics at Notre Dame for roughly seven years. Moreover, Gene was aware of my frustrations and, quite frankly, the unfortunate set of "behind the scenes" circumstances at Notre Dame.

KEVIN M. WHITE, Ph.D.

> **Within college athletics, particularly as a leader, one lives within a proverbial glass house where your professional life is read like an open book.**

However, there are often highly relevant details hidden from public consumption. Gene held the unique position of being privy to the omissions in this particular story. As an industry icon, he was plugged into every potential opportunity within the college athletics marketplace.

Over the years, I have liberally referred to our business as "spaghetti"—leaders, programs, and situations are all intertwined to the point that it can be impossible to detangle. Gene fully understood this crazy phenomenon called spaghetti like no one else in the industry. Therefore, most ironically, as the individual that literally brought me to Notre Dame, Gene was also the one to formally suggest that I might consider other options moving forward. Needless to say, a considerable number of large public institutions expressed an interest in me throughout 2006-2007—several directly, others via a search entity, and a couple through my long-time mentor and confidant, Papa Gene.

At each and every turn, there was some formal conversation happening at Notre Dame about offering me a contract extension. It always became terribly challenging to seriously think about separating from Notre-Dame as an Irish Catholic from New York that emanated from Shamrock Dry Cleaners. Notre Dame had become so tied to our identity, and many members of our extended family, including my favorite Uncle Jimmy O'Donnell, counted on their annual fall pilgrimage to Shamrock Hills in order to experience an overdose of Fighting Irish Football. However, the Duke overture was quick and straightforward. Gene aptly portrayed it as just the right place for me to transition. According to Gene, Duke had a president who was fully committed to athletics and a tremendous history in athletics, all in addition to being a top ten academic institution domestically as well as a top fifteen institution globally. Gene also enthusiastically insinuated that Durham, North Carolina, would be the perfect location for the last chapter of our professional life.

Richard Riddell, Duke's vice president and university secretary, was co-chair of the AD search/selection committee along with Roy Bostock, Duke Board of Trustees Emeritus and a former Duke Football player. Gene directed me to travel to the Hyatt Grand Center at Grand Central Station, NYC, on Thursday, May 29, whereby I was escorted to meet President Brodhead for an extended conversation. On Friday morning, Richard Riddell met me in the lobby, and we walked several blocks to the Chrysler Building offices of the Partnership for a Drug-free America, of which Roy Bostock was chairman. The conversation with Dick Brodhead went on for hours, although I was mindful that that very evening back in Shamrock Hills, South Bend, IN, Jane and I were hosting the annual Notre Dame Monogram Club reception dinner on the side lawn at our home. This event was typically attended by several hundred former ND student athletes, among select others from the university.

As I arrived back home that afternoon, our yard was percolating with music and a tremendous crowd. Unbeknownst to Jane or me, the alumni association, headed by rockstar director, the late Chuck Lennon, had arranged to bring all five of our kids home in addition to many ADs that had been on our staff over the years as a surprise for later that night, Jane and I were awarded as honorary Notre Dame alumni, whereby acceptance speeches were called for with zero anticipation or forewarning. Although the timing was awkward as hell, it was an immensely proud, highly memorable moment for both Jane and me.

Kevin White as Vice President and Director of Athletics at Duke University from May 30, 2008, until his retirement on September 1, 2021.

The party blazed on until it dwindled down to our immediate family all gathered in the kitchen along with a few former staffers who were now ADs at other schools. Around the table, the conversation turned to, *how the hell do we transition to Duke after being so honored and blessed by Notre Dame tonight?* I remember vividly that Mike White popped up and rather candidly said that we should consider tonight a going away party. He said, "It's time to go!" And he was right, yet it was one of the most conflicted positions in which we have ever found ourselves. To top it off, our youngest, Mariah, was going to be a rising senior at St. Joseph's High School in South Bend. Heart-wrenching and painful, to say the least.

Of course, the timing was further complicated: Dick was prepared to send a private plane early on May 30 to take us to Durham, whereby I would speak briefly to the entire AD search committee before the press conference was facilitated that afternoon. Unfortunately, on June 1, 2008, there was a scheduled funeral service at Colby College in Waterville, Maine, for Harold Alfond, who, as you might remember, was like a surrogate father to me as well as a major benefactor at Maine. Duke was terrifically understanding as I spelled out my obligation to attend, and they graciously worked out the travel accommodations to get us to Waterville in a timely fashion. Those four days had to be the most harrowing of our rather intense professional life to date.

Through early June, we spent time buttoning up responsibilities in South Bend while beginning to understand the depth of the challenges in Durham. Making contact with all parties within the department and all over campus, not to mention, benefactors, and a host of others became a way of life over the next several months, and beyond. Transitions can be all consuming within college athletics, for there are endless constituencies to meet, relationships to form, future prospects to be imagined, all in addition to the daily administrative duties associated with the role.

There were a few other challenging dimensions as well: I had just accepted an invitation to be the president of NACDA (National Association of Collegiate Directors of Athletics) as the director of athletics at Notre Dame having just finished my term as president of the Division IA Athletics Director's Association. In addition, I had agreed to assume the directorship/leadership of SMI (Sports Management Institute) that winter (2007/2008). The founder—current University of South Carolina AD, Mike Magee (former USC and Cincinnati AD, Duke and ECU football coach) asked if I would assume his leadership role with his immediate retirement looming. The pivot to me made some sense because Notre Dame was one of the five founding members of SMI. Upon my move to Duke, wherein Duke was not a founding member, other leadership plans were rightfully facilitated.

Suffice to say, the early summer of 2008 was more than a little crazy. For in addition to all of the activity as stated above, during my transition to Duke, I was halfway through my second commitment to the South Bend Homeless Center and to the South Bend Boys and Girls Club, wherein I had agreed to run 1K miles over 100 days and to journal this activity in concert with domestic and global considerations. Not unlike my first "Forrest Gump" run, we had financial commitments approaching $185K, so this obligation needed to be fulfilled. Loved this experience, and the warm reaction from both organizations was life changing.

Flashback two years to 2006: I was pulling weeds in my garden back in South Bend, and I was, not unlike all senior athletics administrators, totally captivated by the ongoing chaos about what has now been historically branded as "Duke Lacrosse." To say that this alleged circumstance captured national imagination and keen interest would indeed be an understatement. Consequently, as I found myself transitioning to Duke in early June of 2008, "Duke Lacrosse" continued to be a widely sensitive topic of ongoing discussion. Therefore, my onboarding at Duke was met with innumerable conversations about a nefarious event which happened before I arrived, not unlike my three previous professional transitions. So, in addition to unearthing the culture, meeting all the key players, becoming one with the mission, and creating a future-minded strategic operational plan, it became incumbent on me to fully understand, and be in a position to articulate both facts and related detail per this massive occurrence that transpired just prior to my arrival.

Once again, not unlike my transition to Tulane (John "Hot Rod" Williams), Arizona State (Stevin "Hedake" Smith), and Notre Dame (Kim Dunbar), I frankly assumed the detail per following up a high profile legal/compliance issue. Not sure if this was intentional or not. However, the trend has become terribly palatable for sure. At least at Duke, I, along

Kevin White with Coach Cutcliffe and Nina King on the sidelines. Nina, his trusted advisor at Duke, succeeded him upon his retirement, becoming the first female VP/AD at Duke and the third Black woman to hold the role at a Power Five school.

with the entire free world, was aware of the widely reported criminal case in which three members of the Duke men's lacrosse team were falsely accused of rape. This alleged incident dated back to March 13, 2006, when a North Carolina Central University student attended a party hosted by the two team captains. Without question, the investigation and resolution of the case sparked public discussion around racism, sexual violence, media bias, and due process on campuses. The former lead prosecutor, Durham County District Attorney Mike Nifong, ultimately resigned in disgrace, was disbarred, and briefly imprisoned for violating ethical standards. Some thirteen months later, on April 11, 2007, North Carolina Attorney General Roy Cooper dropped all charges, declaring the three lacrosse players to be innocent victims of a tragic "rush to accuse" wherein Nifong was described as a rogue prosecutor. Although I never had any direct interaction with those young men, I feel horrible for the three that were falsely accused and their respective families.

During previous transitions, whenever possible, I tried to bring a few critical leaders with me. Jump starting a department, or any organization for that matter, can be an all-consuming "lift."

> **Cultural change is always a significant challenge. Therefore, having a few seasoned leaders with you from the launch can expedite the process significantly. Getting all of the inherited and additive players slotted in the right places, requires a team approach to organizational behavioral change.**

Luckily, there were a few hands raised at Notre Dame expressing a keen interest in transitioning with me to Durham. The three that made the most sense were Stan Wilcox, Boo Corrigan, and Nina King.

Stan came to Duke as the deputy athletic director. Stan was a Notre Dame graduate and former men's basketball student-athlete and associate commissioner of the Big East before joining my staff at ND. Post Duke, he went on to serve as vice president and director of athletics at Florida State before becoming the executive vice president of the NCAA. Boo Corrigan served Duke as senior associate athletic director for external affairs, just as he did at Notre Dame. Boo was also a Notre Dame graduate who moved on to become the vice president and director of athletics at West Point. Today, Boo serves as the vice president and director of athletics at North Carolina State. Nina King transitioned to Duke as chief of staff. Yet another Notre Dame graduate, Nina, has a rich background across several select disciplines at ND and Duke. My professional history with Nina started back in 2000, shortly after I arrived at Notre Dame from Arizona State. I was thrilled to see her most deservingly elevated to vice president and director of athletics at Duke upon my retirement back in 2021.

Armed with this all-star team, we tried to create a reorganization that would complement a strategic plan for the athletics strategy that we inherited entitled, "Unrivaled Ambition." The former AD, Joe Alleva, developed the plan shortly before we arrived. Without question, Duke Athletics facilities had been ignored for many decades. Of course, Cameron Indoor was (and continues to be) a highly coveted cathedral of sorts. Truly, one of the most preeminent venues in the world. However, most other facilities were either non-existent or seriously antiquated/outdated.

As for "Unrivaled Ambition," with some professional assistance, we quickly tried to determine the financial infusion that the strategic plan would warrant. Our initial analysis suggested that, in order to facilitate all of the facility projects projected in the plan, we would conservatively require $500M. In an attempt to mechanize serious forward momentum, both practically and politically, we targeted Roy Bostock (Duke Board of Trustees emeritus member and co-chair of the AD search team that brought me to Duke) to be our supreme leader. Roy became the chair of what was called the "Bostock Group"—right out of the movie, *Father's Day* with Billy Crystal and Robin Williams, "what are the chances of that happening?!"

At the risk of sounding a bit cynical, within the environment at most private elite institutions, there exists a tug-of-war with regard to investing significant resources, whether they are warranted, or not, into athletics. Roy—a recovering trustee whose better half, Merilee, was a major benefactor to the library—possessed political acumen and historical background learned from over six decades and four generations of family relations in athletics. So, with Dick Brodhead's unqualified support and Roy Bostock's indelible skill set and tenacity, along with our elite fundraiser, everyone's favorite "Doberman", Tom Coffman (deputy athletic director for development), Duke Athletics embarked on a $250M campaign within the parent $4.5B university campaign (Duke Forward).

The good news is that because of the Bostock brand and network, and Tom's hard work, Duke Athletics raised approximately $370M, surpassing the stated goal by roughly $120M! The bad news is that unfortunately, not all projects duly specified within Unrivaled Ambition could be financially addressed. That said, with Dick Brodhead's successor as president, Vince Price, along with the talented leader and counselor, Nina King, anything and everything is indeed possible in the next iteration of Duke Athletics; the torch has been successfully passed and change has a real chance of being implemented. Nina King's appointment represents a serious upgrade, for her contemporary outlook coupled with her futuristic vision is perfectly compatible with her extremely talented group of seasoned and next generation administrative and coaching rock stars!

Needless to say, media also plays a crucial role in supporting and advancing athletic programs today. Throughout all of my previous stops, including my most recent tenure at Notre Dame where I renegotiated two different NBC contracts, I continued to grow within the ever-evolving TV landscape. So, when ACC Commissioner John Swofford invited me to serve as the ACC TV Chair shortly after arriving at Duke, I was elated. From the start, one of our core directives as a committee was to secure a broadcast property arrangement which included a conference channel. Suffice to say, after nearly a decade of negotiations, most of which will remain stories for another day told over a glass of red juice, the ACC Network launched with ESPN in 2019, further securing the conference as a leader within Division I athletics. To be sure, this pivotal moment within the ACC and the greater collegiate athletics landscape continues to be a leadership moment of which I remain exceedingly proud to have been a part of.

Kevin White speaking at the Atlantic Coast Conference (ACC) Network Launch.

As I reflect on my early days at Duke, I often chose to schedule all respective meetings within the bleachers at Cameron Indoor Stadium. The vibe is distinctly spirited and celebratory, which made all futuristic considerations instantly palatable. To be honest, CIS is not an amazing, contemporary, architecturally superior home court. However, because of Coach Mike Krzyzewski's phenomenal tenure at Duke, the rafters are littered with championship banners which propel Cameron to be widely held as an epic venue. Sitting in those bleachers fills the senses with an electric energy. When Vince Price arrived at Duke, he referred to Duke Men's Basketball as an American treasure; the program has never been described better.

If Coach K's success has made Cameron utterly iconic, it makes it most difficult to find the proper syntax to describe this one-in-a-hundred generational leader! What Mike has accomplished is simply "mind boggling," and it will never, ever occur again! Yet, five national championships

Kevin White, Chair of the NCAA Division I Men's Basketball Committee, leading the 2020 tournament selection during the COVID-19 pandemic.

don't even begin to account for Mike Krzyzewski's Camelot tenure that even Disney would struggle to embellish. Beyond Duke, Mike's improbable domination of USA basketball accounts for a hand-full of books by itself. He has achieved eleven championships on several world stages, while always finding a way to utilize sport as connectivity to our esteemed military. The Coach K story is without boundaries, from the Emily K Center to the Duke Children's Hospital, to his unrelenting efforts and leadership around the Jimmy V Foundation. However, with all that said, and quickly accounted for, Mike's biggest accomplishment has been the dramatic emergence of Duke University. When Mike and Mickie Krzyzewski arrived in Durham back in the early '80s, Duke was, solidly speaking, a tremendous regional university. Now, Duke is indeed an elite private institution with a peerless domestic and global brand. Of course, there are other elements of Duke that contributed mightily to this elevation, but with limited objectivity, I would argue vehemently that Duke Basketball and Duke Health have been the upwardly mobile catalysts within the modern era.

Kevin White and Coach K honor Dick and Cindy Brodhead for their transformative contributions to Duke University. Dick Brodhead served as the university's 9th president from 2004 to 2017.

Conversely, Duke Football had been struggling for decades. There were just a few moments wherein a heartbeat could be detected—moments when Coach David Cutcliffe did what all others perceived to be the impossible. With a negative brand and a program under-resourced well below any layperson's comprehension (which I must accept some responsibility for), David worked his magic. David arrived in December of 2007 and I came in June of 2008. Coach Cut and I were together briefly at Notre Dame before David took ill and stepped away; and we also knew each other via the Manning family from our time at Tulane. Coincidentally, while David was head coach at Ole Miss, our son was the point guard. On occasion, we would see David at the Catholic mass in downtown Oxford. Arriving at Duke with David in hand was a sizable influence for me. To that end, David did not disappoint—eventually winning the ACC Coastal Division, winning ten games, and making Duke Football

Kevin White cheering on the football team, showing his support and enthusiasm from the locker room.

once again part of the broader NFL enterprise. This upward trajectory was truly invigorating for the entire Duke community. Academically speaking, David's team led the nation in all categories. In addition, he and Karen became ultra-assets to all things Duke; they spent time traveling, speaking, and building relationships with key benefactors who contributed to that $370M campaign mentioned earlier. Loved my thirteen years with both David and Karen, wherein the program was elevated like crazy!

In addition to men's basketball and football, we enjoyed plenty of women's basketball and Olympic sport success too, winning a record number of National Championships and ACC Championships. Just like we did at Notre Dame, we made it a priority to develop an environment in which student-athletes lead both on and off the field. The student-athletes at Duke are outstanding academically, athletically, and socially. Beyond every-

Kevin White with John Swofford, fourth Atlantic Coast Conference (ACC) commissioner, and David Cutcliffe, Duke football coach from 2008 to 2021.

thing they do on campus, they also serve the greater community. Through programs like the Rubenstein Student-Athlete Civic Engagement Program (ACE), they also travel to many countries and provide a wide variety of services to populations who are in need of aid.

During my thirteen years at Duke, I was also deeply involved in two major appointments. Both invitations occurred in 2016, wherein I seriously considered accepting only one. However, upon struggling in that regard, I visited with both the NCAA Division I Men's Basketball Committee and the USOPC separately to indicate that I truly wanted to accept both invitations. I promised I would be diligent per fulfilling each set of responsibilities, and they both enthusiastically agreed.

As a member of the NCAA Division I Men's Basketball Committee, I immediately found the NCAA staff—with the unparalleled leadership of senior vice president, Danny Gavitt—both compelling and riveting. Danny surrounded himself with a star-studded ensemble, including JoAn Scott (Managing Director and recovering Nike executive), a.k.a. "Mother Superior." JoAn ran the day-to-day show, conducting the symphony. Most ironically, I knew Danny through the broader network of our crazy business, but I had never worked with him directly. However, I knew his father, the late Dave Gavitt, fairly well. Almost immediately, I could see that the apple didn't fall far from that highly distinguished tree. Danny could effectively lead any organization with both flair and serious intellect. To be sure, Danny Gavitt is a leader's leader!

My five-year term on the committee flew by, as we had several outstanding chairs supplemented by a group of highly distinguished athletics directors as committee members. Clearly, a remarkable experience, centered on mutual respect, inordinate work ethic, a discernible division of labor, high ethical standards, unqualified integrity, and a promise to leave all self-interest at the committee room door—this was non-negotiable.

Supporting my NCAA Men's Basketball (MBB) Committee work, a SWAT team was formed back on Duke's campus. During my term as committee chair, the SWAT team was a group of staffers that met every Monday morning. They poured over the status of all the Division I teams. The SWAT chair was Billy Zarzour, who at one point worked in and basically ran our office. Billy brought this close-knit group together to do God's work at an exceedingly high level. They continue a group chat until this day; this group felt like they really ran the entire men's basketball tournament selection process. Very prideful. Crazy collegiality and ownership! It was very enjoyable for me to spend an inordinate amount of time with this group each week.

Jane and Kevin White enjoying the game.

In 2019, Bernard Muir (director of athletics at Stanford) became the chair, and I was made Bernard's vice chair. The vice chair becomes the chair the following year, which denotes the historical pattern. This turn in events felt like a "reversal" in a previous professional life role, for Bernard served as my senior associate athletic director at Notre Dame earlier in his distinguished career. Supporting Bernard that year was most fulfilling, for a variety of reasons.

My trip up to the plate as chair eventually became formalized the following year (2020). To be painfully honest, I was proud and terribly excited to lead the group in 2020. Along the way, I had taken mental notes and reaped several tournament-related friendships, whereby it would have been my extreme pleasure to serve the tournament in 2020. It was to be the eighty-second year of the NCAA Men's Basketball Tournament. Of course, as history would now attest, the pandemic got in the way.

With growing concern about the continued advancement of COVID-19, on March 12, at 12:28 p.m., Danny Gavitt and I endeavored to lay out all the facts (as we knew them at that moment). In turn, I asked for a motion to shut down the 2020 Men's Basketball Tournament. Although fuzzy, I believe Mitch Barnhart, vice president and director of athletics at Kentucky, made the motion. And if I remember correctly, Jimmy Phillips, provided a second. It was then a unanimous decision. In turn, Danny and I went to an adjacent hotel room to call Mark Emmert and the NCAA Board. The entire MBB Committee was stunned, frozen. Although there was no alternative, that decision cut deep and will remain with all of us forever. We sat in the selection room motionless for three hours until we asked our esteemed staffer, Tammy Lee, to order some dinner. When the dinner arrived, nobody had an appetite—the mood was seventeen standard deviations below somber.

Members of the NCAA's IT (Information Technology) team (including Colin Chappel) and NCAA statisticians were also in New York at the time the NCAA Men's Basketball Championship was cancelled. With the food being entirely ignored, at roughly 6:00 p.m., I issued my final chair directive: we were all going to O'Lunney's Bar in Times Square, on 45th Street. The proprietor, Hugh O'Lunney, owned and operated this pub since Jesus was in junior high. Hugh came over from Ireland in his teens, working menial jobs around the pub as he worked his way up the food chain; once he saved up all his earnings, he bought the pub on 45th Street. At least one of the committee members indicated that they would prefer to pass on the Irish pub detail and wasn't interested in having a Guinness. My silly retort as the leader of this Titanic-like moment was that everyone was indeed going (no exceptions), and that after our first Guinness, there might well be a second. With COVID looming large, there were very few humans in Times Square, where we took our last team photo. It was indeed eerie, yet it was

MBB Committee Times Square COVID-19 Cancellation 2020

also the greatest collection of comrades ever assembled, which typifies the NCAA Men's Basketball Committee. Hugh O'Lunney died not long ago, at like ninety years old. Bottom line: COVID cancelled the 82nd MBB Tournament, closed O'Lunney's (historic) Irish Pub, and took Hugh, all in one horrific pandemic breath. Ironic. Profound. Sad as hell.

Closing out my reflections on my savored NCAA Division 1 Men's Basketball Committee tenure, perhaps the most richly poignant moment that I will never forget is: right after we made the decision to turn the lights out on the 2020 tournament, Mitch Barnhart, then vice chair and slated to become chair in 2021, emotionally offered to step aside so that I might return to enjoy the entire championship experience. With zero hesitation, I thanked my esteemed colleague profusely, only to watch him most successfully lead the next campaign in 2021. Never have I been so touched by a colleague. It's not surprising that Mitch is widely considered best in class!

My other ancillary appointment while at Duke was to participate as a member of the United States Olympic and Paralympic Committee (USOPC) board, having been identified by the nominating committee chair: Dave Ogren, the USA Hockey CEO and one of the original ESPN principals. It began with a cold call back in 2015 to gauge my level of interest. Over the next fifteen months or so, I took part in several interview sessions, finally to be appointed in March 2016. Of course, as a recovering track coach as well as a staunch advocate for Olympic sports generally speaking, I was euphoric!

Early within my tenure, it was determined that it might make sense to create a Collegiate Advisory Council (CAC) so the USOPC could better connect with the NCAA. To that end, I, along with then Big 12 commissioner, Bob Bowlsby, selected a ten-member committee to support an emerging USOPC unit, "Collegiate Partnerships" yet to be created. The goal was to not only support but enhance the Olympic movement within the greater NCAA landscape. Superstar, Sarah Wilhelmi was recruited to head up "collegiate partnerships," which provided direct support for the CAC, along with the ongoing support of the USOPC CEO, Sarah Hirshland.

The CAC, along with key senior NCAA leaders (in particular, Stan Wilcox and Jenn Frazier), helped remove and/or modify a few NCAA legislative impediments that had negatively impacted the elite athlete community for decades.

It is important to note here that Team USA is the only Olympic enterprise in the world that does not realize federal (government) financial support. As it happens, just over 80 percent of Team USA, current and former, are a product of NCAA institutional programming, coaching, facilities, etc. And it should not be lost on folks that around 40 percent of the Paralympic Team emanates from precisely the same support system. Consequently, branding, if not protecting Olympic sports became the laser focus of the CAC!

This summer, at the Paris Olympics, it was re-invigorating to see the "Olympians Made Here" campaign in action! The brilliant leadership team of the USOPC (in conjunction with the CAC and select NCAA leadership, notwithstanding Team USA) succeeded in producing the greatest show on earth—even during these highly political, turbulent times facing college athletics.

During my term on the Board, I very much enjoyed the distinct opportunity to raise my hand relative to surfing becoming an Olympic sport. It was both an honor and a thrill to watch the surreal competition at the Tokyo Games in 2020 whereby Melbourne, Florida's very own Caroline Marks competed in the first Olympic surfing event and finished fourth. Then, fast-forward to 2024—and Caroline's stunning performance won Gold for Team USA! The Melbourne community has been dear to us since we purchased our condo here in 2002, and our beach has been the sacred gathering place for all of our kids and grandkids every summer since.

In December of 2022, I completed my service on the USOPC. Fortunately, I was able to remain on the USOPC board for two four-year terms. Those eight years clearly represent a very gratifying period within my almost half a century career, whereby I was exceedingly honored to serve Team USA—the pinnacle of American and global sport. During my tenure, there was no shortage of sizable issues or considerations. From the Nasser case, to games postponement, to a leadership transition, to always grappling with financial challenges, my eight-year term was never boring.

Jane and I have loved our intimate association with the Olympic movement, especially being on board with the USOPC in Rio de Janeiro, Brazil (2016), and Pyeongchang, South Korea (2018). Back during our time at Notre Dame, we were also guests of NBC at the Games in Sydney, Australia (2000), Salt Lake City, Utah (2002), Athens, Greece (2004), and Turin, Italy (2006). And at Duke, we were most fortunate to attend the Beijing, China, Olympics (2008), and the London, Great Britain Olympics (2012), both following USA Basketball (via Coach Mike Krzyzewski).

Finally, one last experience outside of Duke Athletics to be forever savored and cherished, occurred upon receiving an unanticipated missive in January 2017 from *Irish America*, inviting us to a Hall of Fame event at the Yacht Club in NYC on March 12, 2017, whereby I was duly inducted and asked to speak. To be honest, given the recent NCAA MBB Committee (2016) and the USOPC (2016) appointments, I was simply overwhelmed, and I had zero knowledge of *Irish America* or the event. Yet, as we got closer to the date, I was told by the CEO, Patricia Harty, that General Martin Dempsey would introduce me and that I would be provided with eight to ten minutes to speak.

The Yacht Club was at capacity, and my four other Irish American Hall of Fame inductees within the class of 2017 were intimidating, for they warranted induction consideration far more than I, a recovering track coach turned athletics administrator. These individuals clearly impacted the broader society at the highest levels. As if I wasn't already uncomfortable, Marty Dempsey introduced me in song! And Marty can really sing—he borrowed the melody but wrote the lyrics.

Jane and I were also blown away by the surprise attendance of Rick and Nina King, our long-standing colleagues and closely-held family friends. As my trepidation elevated, Gerry Adams, former president of Sinn Fein, walked through the door as I attempted to gather my emotional reaction to Marty's masterful crooning.

> **My intent, not unlike I stated at the beginning of this book, was to celebrate my ancestral background, utilizing this terribly unique platform to endeavor to perpetuate both my parents and grandparents.**

Of course, being in this room with all of these well-heeled Irish Americans, I couldn't help myself; I slipped into a little speak relative to my own political inclination, which I realize isn't a universally held sentiment.

> Off the cuff, without any forethought, I suggested that "If there was a wall east of Ellis Island, I wouldn't be speaking with you in this room today, and none of you would be here either." That *Irish America* induction moment has endured most proudly for me, our robust family, and our ancestral family. But, to a greater degree, I am even more proud of being a truth teller!

Retiring from Duke was the most difficult professional decision that I ever had to make. As I embarked on my forty-seventh year in higher education, including teaching, coaching, and administration, it was simply the right time to step aside and provide a distinct opportunity for both new and different voices, and a more contemporary vision.

To be sure, I have been so lucky to serve a number of world class institutions, a zillion terribly gifted student-athletes, the very best coaches in the business, amazing administrative teams, and highly successful departments, as well as countless benefactors and fans while being most graciously supported by fellow faculty and staff colleagues—specifically, eight college and university presidents. Given that, I must convey a special thank you to Dick Brodhead, who very generously invited me to serve Duke University, and to Vince Price, who could not have been more supportive or personally accommodating when he inherited this senior citizen as vice president and director of athletics.

Professionally speaking, I have been mentored by a phenomenal set of "tutors" along the way: Gene Corrigan, Cedric Dempsey, Roy Kramer, Joe

Kearney, Homer Rice, Don Canham, as well as so many others... would certainly be a painfully long list... point is, Jane and I have been extremely fortunate, well beyond words.

As I continue to follow the yellow-brick road toward the future of college athletics, now as a consultant for Huron, one thing that is steadfastly certain is that the corporate America model characterized within my MBA Sports Business class over the past four decades is alive and well. If you're still with me, please indulge some well-intended prognostications from a long-time practitioner, vice president/director of athletics emeritus, and Fuqua School of Business professor in the next chapter.

CHAPTER 10

A RADICAL SHIFT: REIMAGINING THE FUTURE OF COLLEGE ATHLETICS

"Even if the last move did not succeed, the inner command says move again."

SEAMUS HEANEY

When I think privately about this challenging moment within the world of college athletics, I hear these words emanating from the great American poet, Bob Dylan: "There must be some way outta here, said the joker to the thief. There's too much confusion, I can't get no relief…"

> When I first stalked/approached Dr. Marsh back in New Port Richey in 1973, sport was a far different enterprise to say the very least. Several things have underscored my reflective thinking as I am no longer "in play," and currently reside up in the clubhouse.

First, the size and scope of sport—once again, an economist colleague back in 2015, prophesied that sport domestically represents approximately 6.1

percent of the GDP, or $985B annually; and globally, like $3T (Trillion) annually, or 4.7 percent of the world economy. Moreover, just thinking about our own philanthropic activity at the six institutions we were most fortunate to serve, we easily raised just over $1B for scholarships, operations, and facilities. It's hard to fathom!

Of course, as the world class historian, James Michener, detailed in *Sport in America* back in 1976, sport, and/or college athletics specifically, would indeed futuristically emulate the American business modalities. In terms of college athletics, traditional conferences would be replaced with consortiums, which would manage/oversee championships, negotiate broadcast property agreements, etc., and geography and historic rivalries would become far less critical. If I may paraphrase—as Michener thought about other major economic sub-sectors, college athletics would become just another economic juggernaut that it would find its own way forward (today, referred to as conference realignment) to amortize more resources across fewer units. Back in the late '60s and early '70s those trends within the banking community, airlines, telecommunications, and auto industry were just taking form.

Once again, there are drivers within the system that are dictating behaviors which are not readily or easily understood by participants, decision makers, or spectators around the business of sport. All of the aforementioned forces have produced a departure from yesteryear's model wherein a scholarship component along with select infrastructure considerations satisfied the terms of agreement relative to the student-athlete experience. Over the past decade, NCAA rules and regulations have become far more permissive, and the investment per matriculating student-athletes has been substantially increased. With the elevation of broadcast property income, philanthropy, and traditional income, these financial adjustments have been (conservatively) facilitated.

The economics of college athletics has remained fairly constant since *Sport in America* was written back in 1976. Pointedly, the lion-share of revenue within college athletics is derived from football and men's basketball. Incidentally, per every broadcast property dollar generated by college athletics, approximately $.80 is attributable to football and $.20 to men's basketball.

With the arrival of NIL and a few other significant legislative considerations, the economics around college athletics are being re-worked. It should be noted that there are only around twenty Division I institutions that currently enjoy a positive cash flow! Again, upon removing all the gimmicky financing—"funny money" if you will—of the 355 Division I institutions, only about twenty are not dependent on bloated student fees, tuition waivers, state appropriations, non-chargeable institutional costs, etc. Should you think in terms of the entire 1,100 membership cohort of the NCAA (all divisions), the case as depicted above becomes far more dire.

As for Division II and Division III, any permissiveness and/or accommodations that apply to Division I should also apply to the other sub-divisions as well, especially mental health and degree completion benefits, for they will require direct membership subsidization. And, as I've said before, there is strength in numbers. To that end, there are real benefits for Division I to associate with Division II and III, and vice versa.

> **Today, most collegiate athletics programs/departments are financially hemorrhaging! It's a supreme challenge to be a card-carrying member of a competitive cohort and operate unilaterally, which means that spending/investing above your means is a way of life.**

Consequently, because of the institutional advancement benefits, brand enhancement, enrollment, university development, awareness/rankings, appropriations, etc., universities are investing directly into intercollegiate athletics like never before.

All institutions are elevating their athletics franchises! In terms of pursuing an anti-trust exemption, that protection would be highly impactful, for as an association, the NCAA will literally go bankrupt over time due to mounting legal fees. Not to mention, inviting Congress to repair college athletics is akin to being asked to construct a Christmas Eve toy for your child post-midnight without directions. Certainly, Congress has much larger fish to fry than praying over NIL, the transfer portal, and other related regulatory issues.

Looking back at the 118-year history of the NCAA, which began in 1906, there has never been so much noise, criticism, and/or general toxicity. Given that, there are some 1,100 NCAA institutional members endeavoring to accommodate the needs and interests of around 500K student-athletes. In total, there are almost 3K colleges and universities attempting to do "God's work" in that regard. At a sizable number of institutions, the institutional piece of the sport sponsorship equation has trumped the experiential dimension. However, throughout this eclectic spectrum of colleges and universities, there are programs that are more attuned with the student-athlete experience than with branding, institutional philanthropy, elevated awareness which directly impacts enrollment, and all the rest.

Throughout my almost fifty years within education, I have observed an ongoing shift in that regard. There is a tug-of-war between the experience element and the entertainment element (that has been carefully, institutionally speaking, monetized). This is the oversized conundrum facing the modern-day NCAA, which is seriously antiquated, and has always struggled with a lack of homogeneity since its inception. When speaking to this point publicly, I often refer to the bar scene in the movie *Star Wars*.

For not unlike that illustrative scene with varying sizes, shapes, and colors of the uniquely depicted patrons, the NCAA is made up of a rather broad set of members representing big markets, small markets, private schools, public schools, faith-based schools, and so on. Some of these institutions are more committed to the experiential dimension than their counterparts that are heavily focused on the commercial (entertainment driven) objective, which dramatically influences branding, philanthropy, admissions, rankings, legislative support, etc.

> **Today, as American higher education renegotiates its relationship with its long-standing partner, college athletics, it is faced with many new, if not contemporary, headwinds: Title IX, DEI, NIL, House, Alston, the prospective pivot to streaming, as well as serving as a regulatory arm (functionally speaking) per an un-compromised, competitive environment.**

As the NCAA legislates the modernization of the membership objectives, it (rightfully so) has earmarked the need to better understand and remediate mental health; this must take precedence in the future. In addition, post support for ongoing medical assistance as well as degree completion must be a non-negotiable part of the next iteration of college athletics. As previously noted, I have often referred to myself as a "loaves and fishes" director of athletics, yet it is not lost on me that you can only spend a dollar once. Therefore, the financial apparatus to ensure full coverage and access must be deliberated within all financial planning processes.

Quite frankly, in this regard, the university, who is the ultimate beneficiary of all the institutional advancement capital harvested should greatly participate in providing aid for athletes when they are finished playing. This would include support for ongoing medical expenses and degree completion after they no longer have NCAA eligibility. This seems only fair and reasonable to me—simply "the cost of doing business." The university reaps the rewards of student-athlete participation/success (via branding, marketing, rankings, etc.) while they are competing for the university. So, paying for any costs associated with that participation that occur after said participation has ended should fall on the university, at least partially. This would be my working outline moving forward:

1. My first thought is that the NCAA as we know it (within the immediate era), will need to dramatically decentralize. A division of labor will indeed occur, equipping conferences with more everyday oversight, responsibility, etc. One would think that this division of labor might denote that the NCAA would maintain parental oversight, warehousing data while facilitating championships as well as serving as the ultimate custodian of agreed upon rules and regulations; but, in addition, the NCAA must masterfully engage in supreme storytelling, not unlike the Walt Disney variety. In addition, the NCAA will need to be the negotiator of all broadcast property initiatives.

2. Given that vision, I foresee third party/outsourced enforcement, comparable to the IRS relationship with the federal government and/or SafeSport relative to the USOPC.

3. Although there is keen interest to position football even further away from the parent enterprise, I believe that when the community sobers up, that idea will be deemed as only further separating college athletics, if not the sport of football, from the academy. How college football operates at the highest level currently is untenable within a non-reconcilable state, or perhaps better said, it is "on a collision course!"

4. College athletics must remain a core component element within American higher education. In my view, this is absolutely critical. As a recovering non-student—which is code for a poor student who was affected by the ghost of Christmas past in terms of formal education—addressing my educational gap became an obsession late in my journey. Valuing education, in my heart of hearts, I believe is paramount in terms of university and college selection and matriculation, as well as degree completion. There is ample empirical evidence to support this strong position. Attending a college or university is truly a forty to fifty-year decision. The group you throw in with is just who you become.

5. Once again, where a prospective student-athlete attends must continue to matter. As noted above, the community they join should be packaged with a discernible ROI over their respective lifetime. It can't be just about immediate "pay for play." Should that continue unobstructed, it will become the beginning of the end. Some 500K are reliant on this highly unique, leadership development experience. Therefore, it must be maintained and unscathed. This sacred experience provides a critical access mechanism to higher education, especially for first generation students as well as underrepresented populations and the continued advancement of women, who are emerging as a strong leadership dimension of American, if not global, society. College athletics has been the clubhouse leader on all these fronts in terms of access, even overshadowing the GI Bill since WWII. All of the above needs to be celebrated by far better storytelling!

6. It's never been lost on me that the university system, generally speaking, has historically been developed via an equalitarianism mentality. That has been the blueprint on the academic side, and it must continue to be prudent on the athletics side of the ledger as well. Just as multiple sections of freshmen composition (English 101) pay

for metaphysics, football and men's basketball pay for all the Olympic sports. Pointedly, most institutional domains don't cash flow within that traditional financial model. Moreover, by definition, university is a syntax for the word universal, as in the expectation that the needs and interests of all the matriculating constituencies should be accommodated within reason.

7. Although it's almost impossible to legislate human behavior, NIL without guardrails has the real potential to make college athletics as we know it today, particularly in terms of broad sports sponsorship, non-existent. At some point, this permissive, although warranted, potential to earn "legitimate" resource for student-athletes will now live in perpetuity. However, this lawless, unsustainable financial reality may indeed cause an irreconcilable divorce between athletics and its mother ship. Thus, the rather conservative academy is at risk. Not for nothing, the American collegiate model whereby academia and sport coexist is truly a major point of difference for America and the envy of the rest of the world. Many other countries have tried to study and emulate. However, our model is still "one of one!"

Before discussing prospective NIL options to a greater degree, let me simply say that the combination of NIL and the transfer portal may indeed endanger this holy, symbiotic relationship between academics and sport that has enjoyed a 118-year history. Until we have a larger sample size, it would be counter-intuitive to not believe that this (NIL and transfer portal) moment won't drive down graduation rates. No more than a decade or so ago, athletics educators and select others were obsessed with degree completion data and graduation rates—rightly so. The widely articulated notion marketed within that particular era was for a student-athlete to use sport as a vehicle, not to allow sport to use them, which was referred to as basic exploitation.

> As a recovering athletics educator, I find myself consumed with the prospect of pejorative data/outcomes as the latest sample size eventually expands. In my view, this new paradigm will have a terribly high cost. The next chapter of college athletics will be a challenge on many fronts.

Lots of competing forces surround the 500,000 student-athletes who are currently in the system, not counting NAIA and other select groupings, including our esteemed "Team USA."

Therefore, with all of these opinions and expressed concerns keeping me up at night, I was invited to participate in a panel discussion at NACDA (National Association of Collegiate Directors of Athletics) in June of 2022 in Las Vegas. As depicted in the introduction to this manuscript, the panel was put together by the Huron Group, which is where I am hanging a shingle these days. Our panel unapologetically went on for about ninety minutes, wherein I candidly ranted about all of these well inventoried concerns, and I harvested a wide array of colleague responses.

Fast forward to February 2023: I was invited to speak at the national AGB (Association of Governing Boards) convention in San Diego along with Vice Chair of Huron's Board of Directors and Managing Director for Strategy and Operations, Jim Roth. During the panel, I delivered yet another set of candid remarks about the current state of college athletics. Not surprisingly, the conversation broke along similar lines as our discussion in Vegas. Recently, yet another NACDA conversation occurred in June 2023.

Bottom line: there is an acknowledgment that NIL and the transfer portal were adopted with good intention; however, the mayhem, let alone the financial realities are not sustainable. Again, the pool of existing resources around college athletics is pretty well defined. As I often say, the disposable or investment resource pool is already captured/identified. So, over my lifetime, when I observe a re-distribution of existing resources, not accounting for an uptick—there are always winners and losers. My fear is that Olympic sports will eventually be short-sheeted in order to further invest in more commercial sports like football and men's basketball. As a former track coach and recent USOPC board member, I am conditioned to be skittish.

As I close out this chapter, from like 50K feet, not to be confused with the tarmac, I envision three levels of varying gradations to think about NIL futuristically:

A. Fully subscribe to an equalitarian model where all student athletes harvest a consistent, comparable NIL stipend. This would greatly minimize the role of third-party influencers, moving them back out of the game and locker room, while also protecting an institution from Title IX or all other equity related issues. It could even be portrayed as a conservative "pay for play" model. I do understand that former NCAA President, Mark Emmert floated this concept but that it did not realize much support. Once again, NCAA legislation has been terribly permissive over the past decade or so, considering the same would likely require some form of collective bargaining, but it might negate the employee status from becoming a reality, which would be problematic for both the student athletes and the university.

B. A mid-range point might consist of "A" with some rigid guard rails mechanized around acceptable relationships, coupled with the realization of prospective ancillary income. Yes, this may indeed be a legalistic nightmare. However, when an association becomes permissive then tries to become more conservative, the legal buttons are at once enacted.

C. For me, not "play for pay" but "pay to play" exists at the other end of the continuum. The NCAA, as well as all the respective parties, might fully subscribe to the ultimate "free market" system, whereby student athletes, as independent contractors, unionize, and create a wide-open space not unlike the current reality: allowing student athletes to earn as much as the market will bear and, in turn, charge student athletes "sticker price" for their aggregate experience from coaching, to tuition, to all the services and aspects which would be provided. However, there are lots of complications, if not legal migraines, relative to this solution.

Although my modeling may be unrealistic, choosing door A, door B, or door C begins to detail differing levels of compensation and/or support. If you are a traditionalist, not unlike me, and spend a lot of time thinking about new or additional revenue streams within the existing college athletics universe, you might become concerned, as we are now in the throes of redistributing the current pie of resources, and the low hanging fruit has already been harvested. In my humble view, if the pie is the pie, when redistribution occurs, there are always "winners and losers." At the end of the day, Olympic sports will get short-sheeted, whereby Team USA will be severely impacted and/or sidelined.

> Having coached Olympic sports, served on the USOPC board for eight years, and chaired the Collegiate Advisory Council (CAC), to suggest that I am concerned about the future of Olympic NCAA sports is a serious understatement.

Ultimately, to the degree that NCAA Olympic sports are marginalized, Team USA will be severely impacted. As noted in Chapter 9, roughly 80 percent of Team USA consists of current or former NCAA student-athletes, and around 40 percent of the Paralympics Team competes and/or trains on NCAA campuses. The NCAA Olympic sports system operates like a living endowment for Team USA, which is critical to the extraordinarily successful Olympic mission. Remember, once again, the USA system is the envy of the world, for we continue to be the only country with a combined higher education and college athletics option, if not, dual curriculum.

I particularly love the pointed Team USA marketing message, "Olympians Made Here!" This marketing quip was coined by Sara Wilhelmi, USOPC director of collegiate partnerships, with the help of Sandy Barbour, CAC marketing committee chair. As it pertains to college athletics, the message might more aptly suggest, "Leaders Made Here!" This deserves to be highly celebrated, inordinately savored, as well as richly enjoyed by all respective American constituencies.

Regarding the future prospect of employee status for the student-athlete cohort within the confines of the university work force: I cringe about this prospect as a retired practitioner. That said, there are strong philosophical and economical opinions (even considering the advent of taxable income) that are up for further analysis and interpretation. Therefore, this relationship status within the university community may indeed become a reality. In the near term, as a community within higher education, we should focus on the rearview mirror and find the best way to settle outstanding financial commitments to former student-athletes before transitioning to the most beneficial ways to revenue share with current and future student athletes.

Amortizing the rearview mirror while looking at a future financial (revenue share) model will certainly headline all activity over the next several years. Given the unregulated nature of NIL and the transfer portal, coupled with the reality that employment status may indeed become an operational option, it is my opinion that we must harbor unqualified optimism about the future prospects for the institution of college athletics.

> If we lose hope or allow ourselves to become
> too negative, we risk losing one of the greatest
> human development enterprises in the world.

With an emphasis on both *student* and *athlete*, the college athletics community must retain unrelenting pride around the greater college athletics enterprise, which currently supports some 500K incredible student-athlete experiences, unlike any other experiences they might otherwise harvest on a college or university campus. This robust cohort of student-athletes also clearly holds a significant percentage of both first generation and historically under-represented populations.

> Finding my way through the front door of
> college athletics without targeted deliberation
> or prescription has been like winning the life
> lottery. So, whatever happens, I will always
> be truly grateful for this magical journey.

Even though, at this point, almost a half a century later, the greater enterprise looks terribly different to me, I am most appreciative for the opportunity to sit at the bar and quietly reflect on all the trials, tribulations, highs, and lows.

To be pointed, wherein we were able to positively move the needle, we enjoyed strong political alignment. Conversely, in the instances that we didn't harvest the level of desirable and/or expected success, we did a poor job managing the competing political forces. It's that simple!

> My most powerful, if not memorable, reflections contain private thoughts of nurturing and supporting student-athletes while working with an amazing cohort of coaches, staff, senior administrators, board members, faculty, and the benefactor community.

In the interest of eventually getting the train back on the tracks, I personally believe that the greater enterprise needs an infusion of practitioners at the top of the professional food chain. There existed a culture within college athletics for over a century whereby some level of collegiality and working collectively produced this model which has become the envy of the world. My supreme hope is that the larger college athletics community returns to the day when practitioners, once again, really matter.

As an analogy, I think about the empire that is Apple: when they choose a leader to follow the late Steve Jobs, they went with someone from their industry; they appointed a leader from within Apple, Tim Cook. I could make the same case for Jamie Diamond at JP Morgan, Mary Barra at General Motors, and for Adam Silver (NBA) and Roger Goodell (NFL); they were all seasoned leaders with experience around complicated sub-sectors, both politically and practically, within terribly challenging times. In my humble view, taking a risk/going outside the box can be debilitating, particularly within impossible moments of unrest and heightened discourse.

Finally, I may sound like a nostalgic old man, but college athletics during the Camelot years was most effectively led by the likes of Cedric Dempsey, Gene Corrigan, Jim Delany, Tom Hansen, Roy Kramer, Mike Slive, Chuck Neinas, Steve Hatchell, Dave Gavitt, Bob Bowlsby, Mike Tranghese, John Swofford, and the list goes on. All these leaders emerged through a vibrant career within the industry.

Lighting candles that we find our way back to much more agreeable days, for I truly love college athletics and, no matter what happens in the future, I always will! Once again, special thanks for taking this road trip with me. Trust me, I will be forever grateful!

EPILOGUE

> "It's lovely to know that the world can't interfere with the inside of your head."
>
> FRANK MCCOURT, *ANGELA'S ASHES*

The most important things for any higher education administrator to understand regarding athletics is the purpose and goal of college athletics and the student-athlete experience. Throughout my career, I've always seen myself as a servant leader, and since I am not built for full retirement, I still enjoy serving various athletic departments as a consultant with the Huron Group. Once one experiences financial instability, there will never, ever be enough financial resources. But one can take some solace in being able to reshape the preexisting paradigm, while also helping others to do the same.

Over my elongated career, we have worked diligently to help advance talented, aspirational, next generation leaders around college sport. Without denouncing all humility, I can honestly convey that, from our ranks, some thirty-two individuals have become leaders (ADs, commissioners, as well as a president). To be sure, we are incredibly proud that over seventy institutions have been affected by their outstanding leadership. Given that, we are even more proud of the fact that some 30 percent of that esteemed cohort are either female or members of a historically under-represented group. At Duke specifically, the athletic department went from having one female member and no Black or Brown administrators on the senior and executive staff in 2007 to having eight women and four Black and Brown leaders in those roles during our tenure. Furthermore, at four of the five Division 1 colleges/universities where we were at the helm, we had the distinct honor of hiring the first Black head coach. In addition, we developed a program called Open Door Initiative, which allowed for young, Black and Brown emerging professionals to have an opportunity to intern in Duke's athletic administration every summer, giving them a chance to cross the threshold into a world of athletic administration in the future.

> **To be completely unvarnished, we—Jane and I—have been euphoric to represent each and every institution that we have been most fortunate to serve. Without question, we have absolutely loved working alongside a ridiculous number of student-athletes and coaches over all these crazy years. Each stop on this journey has been, in its own way, just a magical experience.**

With that said, the last sixteen years at Duke have been most enjoyable, for the greater Blue Devil family has truly embraced our immediate family, which has embarked almost exclusively on their own career path within education and/or college athletics. In a few words, it's been a wonderful marriage!

At the end of the day, having had the distinct opportunity to combine education and entertainment within the context of sport has not only been terribly gratifying, but also an outgrowth of my ancestral background, where our family has been cited as highly accomplished Irish teachers while remaining deeply engrained in entertainment—be it in traditional sport or music, dance, etc. I am who I am because of my ancestral roots. To that end, I take great pride in being a teacher, a mentor, and a leader, which are all profoundly found within my Irish DNA.

Reflecting on this unique legacy and journey, I find myself relishing the fact that all of our kids are college graduates—four of which have graduate degrees—and as undergraduates attended the likes of Tulane, Ole Miss, Notre Dame, and Duke. The odds of that occurring in my generation were indeed de minimis to say the least. Moreover, to be able to account for four lawyers within our family is also shocking. Not to mention, our unbelievable grandkids coming up now are able to achieve at a pinnacle "fever pitch" level. That's the real stunning thing for me; it is a fascinating element within this immediate sitcom which again brings me back to the "loaves and fishes." They all inherited glorified breadcrumbs and turned them into a seven-course gourmet dinner!

Finally, I must convey a public thank you to my spouse, Jane, with whom I began our athletics career back in 1973 as a highly enthusiastic teaching and coaching duo! Jane was the most athletic person in our family in her day as a runner and as an extremely competitive, talented basketball player before Title IX. And Jane White is legitimately the best high school or college coach I have ever observed firsthand. Lucky for us, long after she retired as a teacher and coach, she has continued to serve as the head coach of our family with a current team roster of twenty-eight!

Now, as I sit on the front porch, aging at an unprecedented rate, my head and heart are consumed with our damn good fortune. Although I've lived a life that suffers from serious imperfection, God has always kept the light on (bright) for me. His constant ray of utter sunshine has strongly encouraged me to "treat others the way in which I'd like to be treated, and to try like hell to do the right thing when nobody's watching." Moreover, I know that I emerged from an amazing bassinet, and I am immensely proud to be a representative of this stellar, although a bit unique, Irish DNA. But more than anything, I suspect that I am the product of being in just the right place at the right time!

ADDITIONAL ACKNOWLEDGMENTS

Heartfelt thanks to my *The Good Sport* team:

My very talented co-author and eldest daughter, Maureen Treadway, B.A. Tulane, M.F.A. Arizona State. Without you, this never would have happened.

My esteemed literary agent, both a Dukie and a Dubliner, Sharon Bowers, Literary Agent, Folio Literary Management.

Our project manager, Darby Nevola, B.A. Northwestern University, a veteran of Duke Athletics administration who originated as the lead Special Assistant for both Nina King and me.

Our venerated editor, John Jardin, Literary Associate, Folio Literary Management, B.S. University of Georgia.

The terrific team at Huron, Tim Walsh, Margaret Stanzell, Nathalie Rock, Ben Wiseman.

For your friendship, guidance, and support along the way (in alphabetical order):

John and Katie Anthony
Sandy Barbour
Charlie and Rebecca Besser
Roy Bostock
Mark Brand
Dick Brodhead
Art Chase
Jim Collins
Jim Delany
Marty and Deanie Dempsey
Mike and Lois Gartland
Dave and Ronda Gartland
Jarett Gerald
John Jardin
Jaz Johnson
Carol Kaesebier
Chris Kennedy
Nina King
Dale Lick
Renie Lynch
Pat Manak
Bishop Martin
Mick and Peg McDonough

Todd Mesibov
Chip Murray
Tom Nevala
Monsignor Hugh O'Donnell
Lisa O'Dwyer
Frank O'Mara
Jim Phillips
Greg Powell
Martha Putallaz
Bob and Eyvonne Ryan
Jim Roth
Juli Schreiber
Phil Schreier
Blair Sheppard
Margaret Stanzell
Randy Sushko
John Swofford
Doug Tamaro
Bob Vecchione
Tim Walsh
Kyle Waterstone
All of our children and grandchildren

ABOUT THE AUTHOR

Kevin White has had a storied career as one of America's most influential athletic directors. From his early days at the University of Maine to leadership roles at Tulane, Arizona State, Notre Dame, and a transformative two-decade tenure at Duke, he has steered some of the most prominent athletic programs in the nation. His achievements include serving on the Board of Directors for the U.S. Olympic Committee, chairing the NCAA Men's Basketball Division I Committee, and earning the respect of countless colleagues and athletes alike. Even while navigating the demands of his career, he pursued academic excellence, earning multiple advanced degrees—including a doctorate—and completing post-graduate studies at Harvard. Today, though retired from Duke, White continues to share his expertise as a faculty member at Duke's prestigious Fuqua School of Business.

White is widely regarded as one of the most experienced and distinguished athletic directors in American sports history. His leadership philosophy—centered on the success and well-being of athletes on and off the field—has earned him unwavering loyalty from those around him. Remarkably, 32 of his former assistants now lead sports programs across the United States. His legacy also lives on through his family: four of his five children hold leadership roles in college athletics, including his sons Mike, head basketball coach at the University of Georgia, and Danny, athletic director at the University of Tennessee. *Sports Illustrated* has fittingly called the Whites "The First Family of Athletic Directors."

Now, in *The Good Sport*, White reflects on his extraordinary 47-year career, offering an unparalleled perspective on the evolution of college athletics. With the 2021 Supreme Court decision reshaping the NCAA's approach to name, image, and likeness (NIL) rights, White takes a candid and critical look at the ongoing chaos, the gaps in legislation, and what it all means for the future of intercollegiate sports. Having played an active role in navigating these issues, White brings a unique and authoritative voice to the debate.

This deeply personal and thought-provoking book is more than a memoir. It's a call to action for leaders across all fields. White confronts the challenges of advancing diversity and inclusion in a historically exclusive profession and shares invaluable lessons about leadership, perseverance, and integrity.

THE GOOD SPORT is a must-read for sports fans, aspiring leaders, and anyone seeking inspiration to do what's right—even when it's difficult. Kevin White's story is a testament to toughness, heart, and the power of principled leadership.